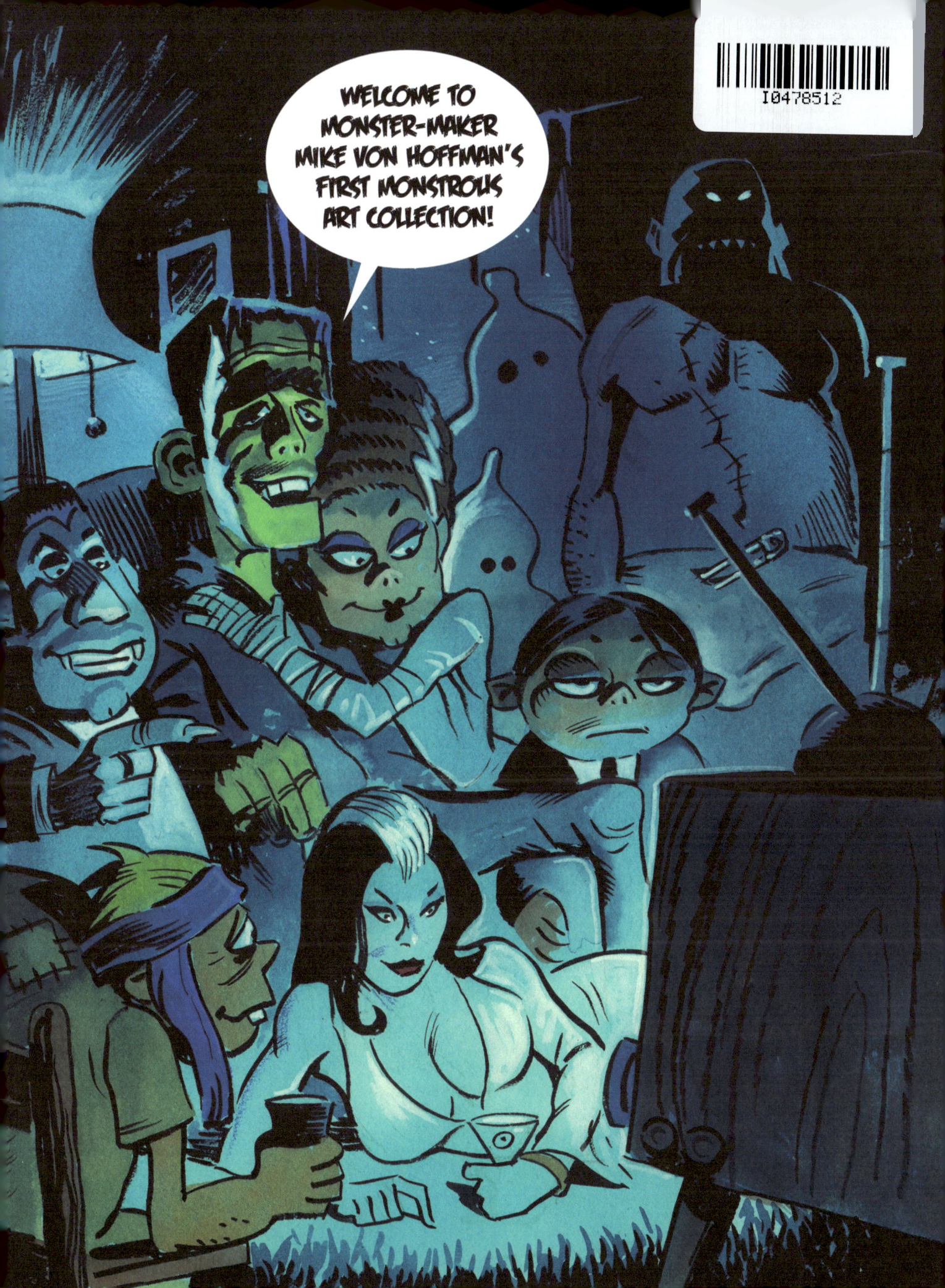

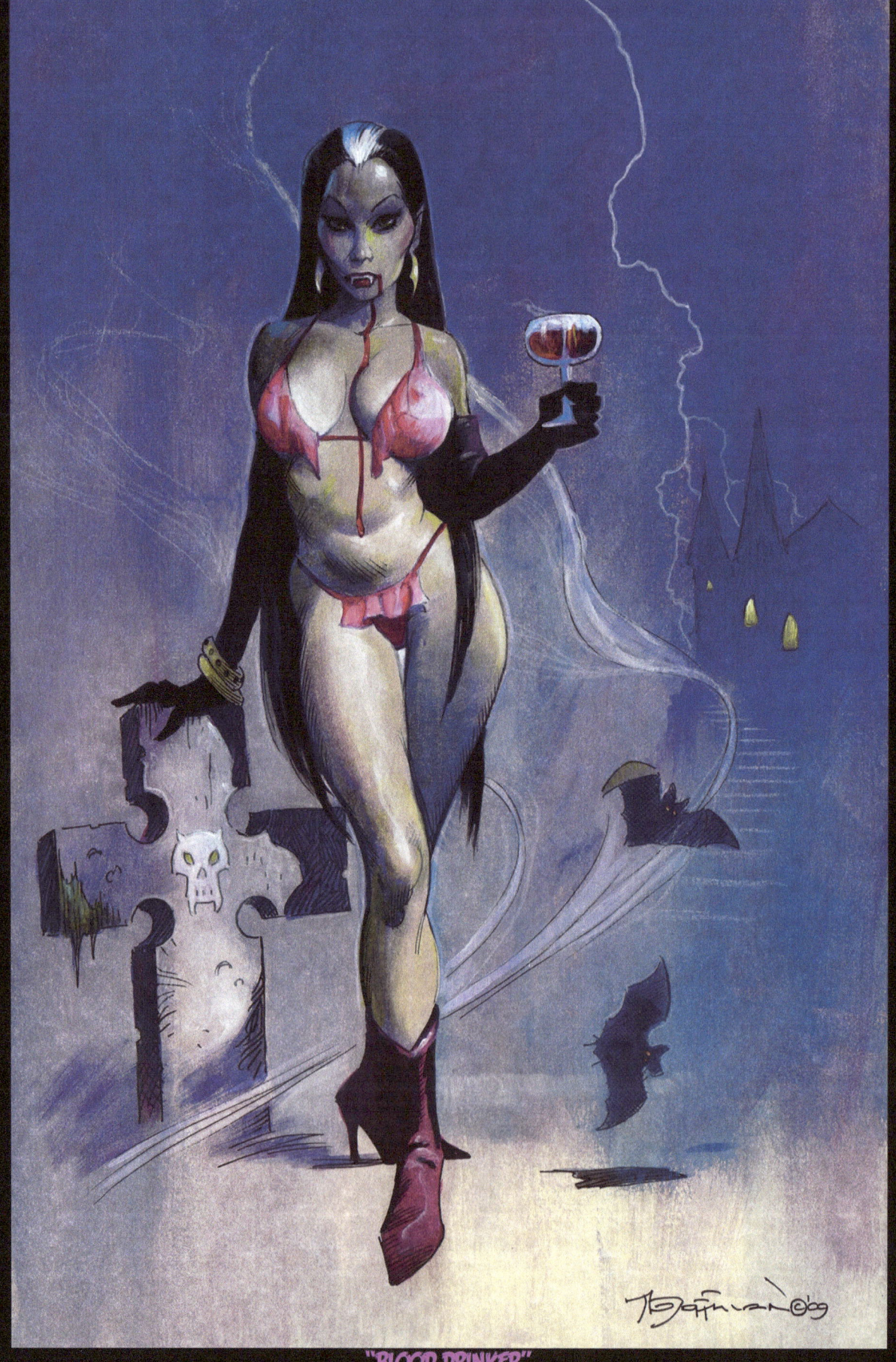

"BLOOD DRINKER"

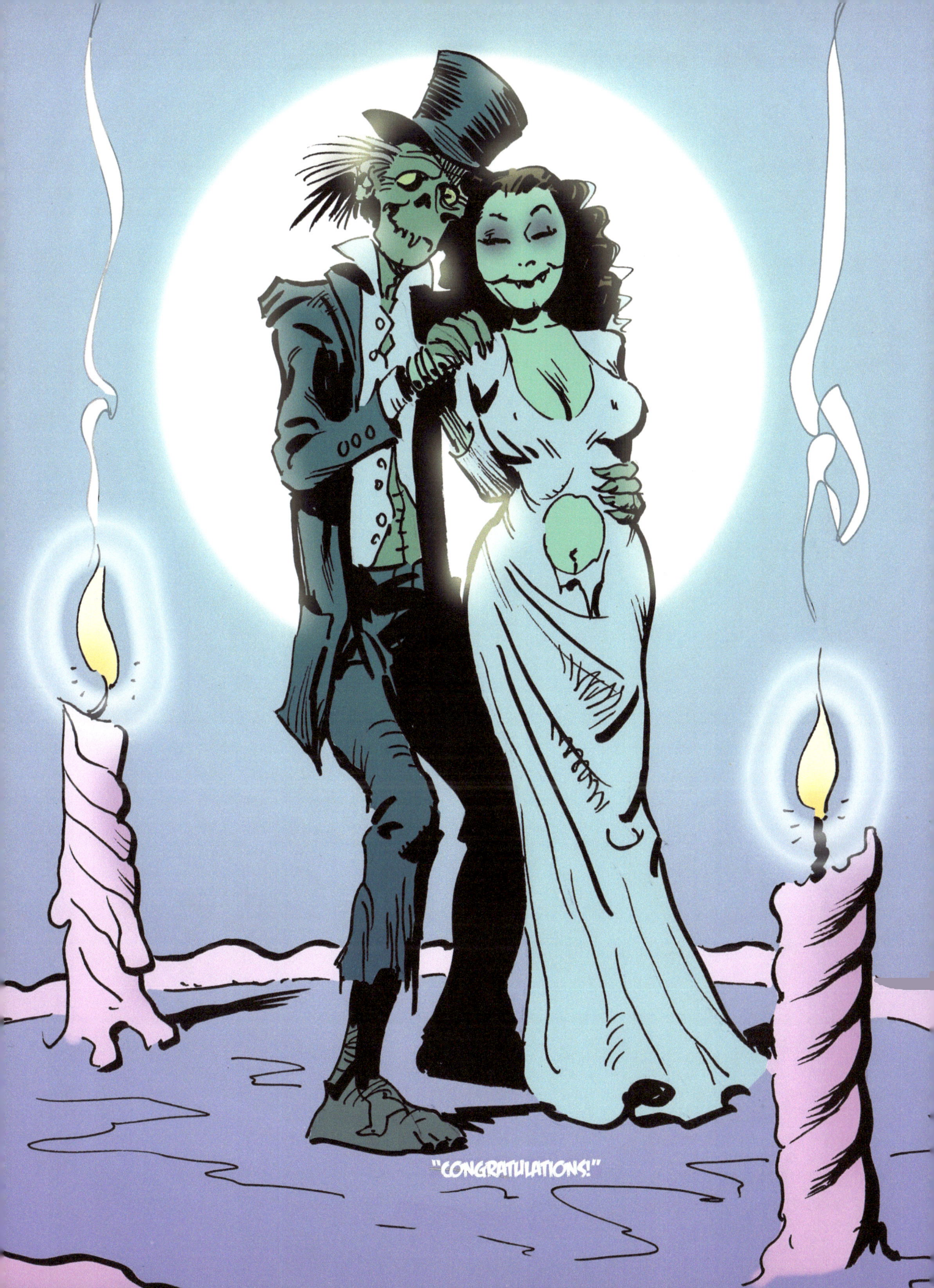

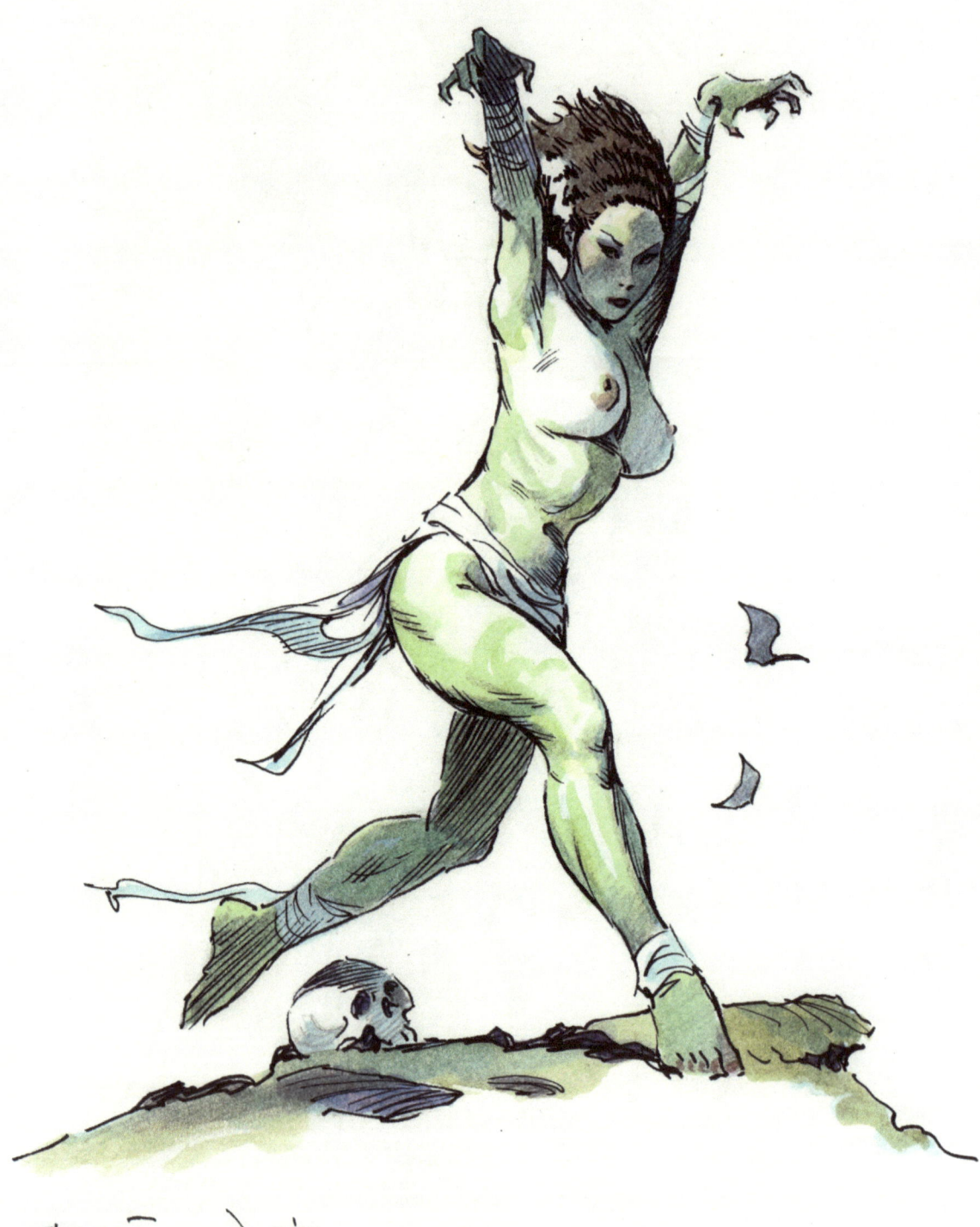

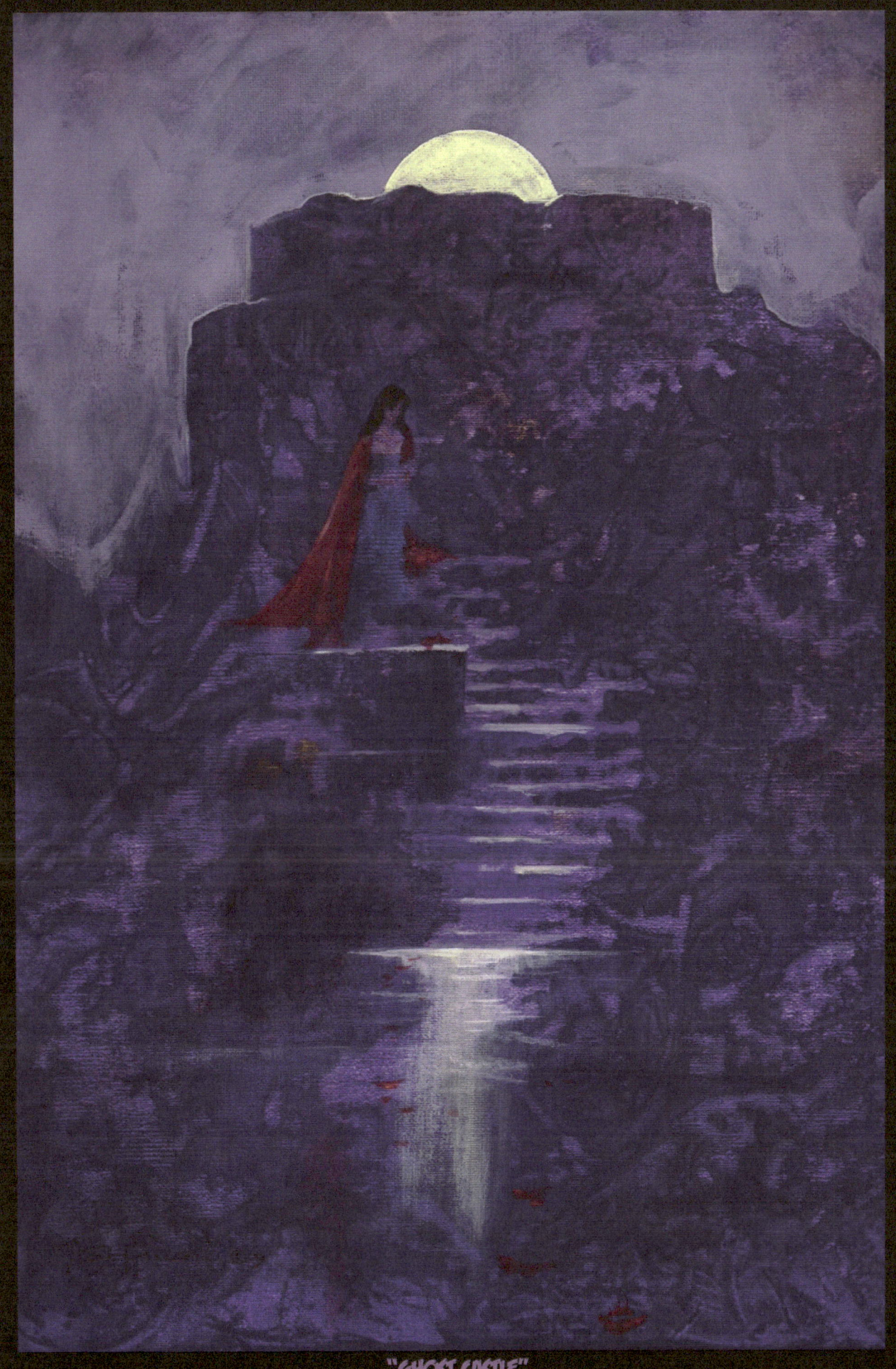

"GHOST CASTLE"

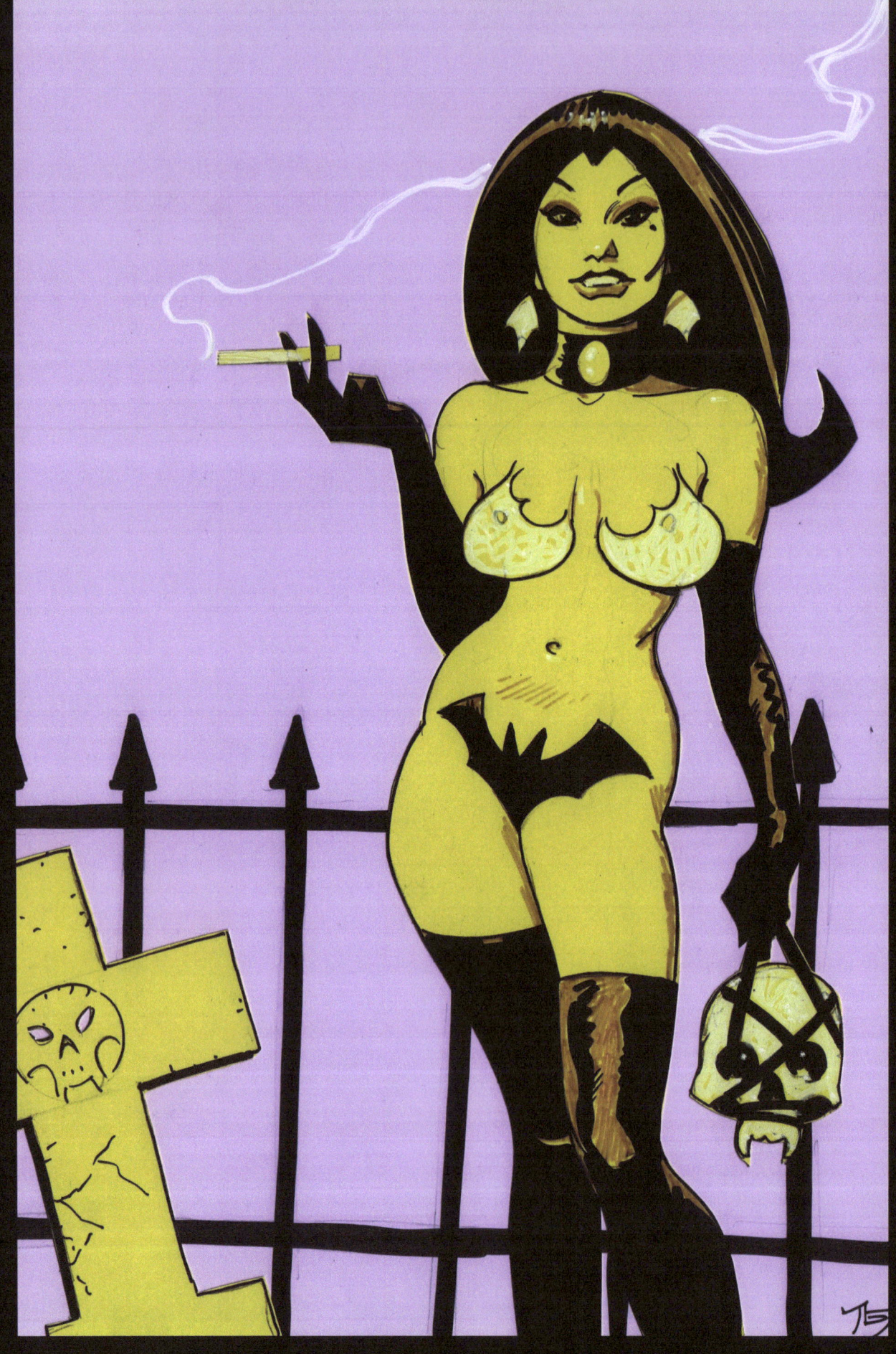

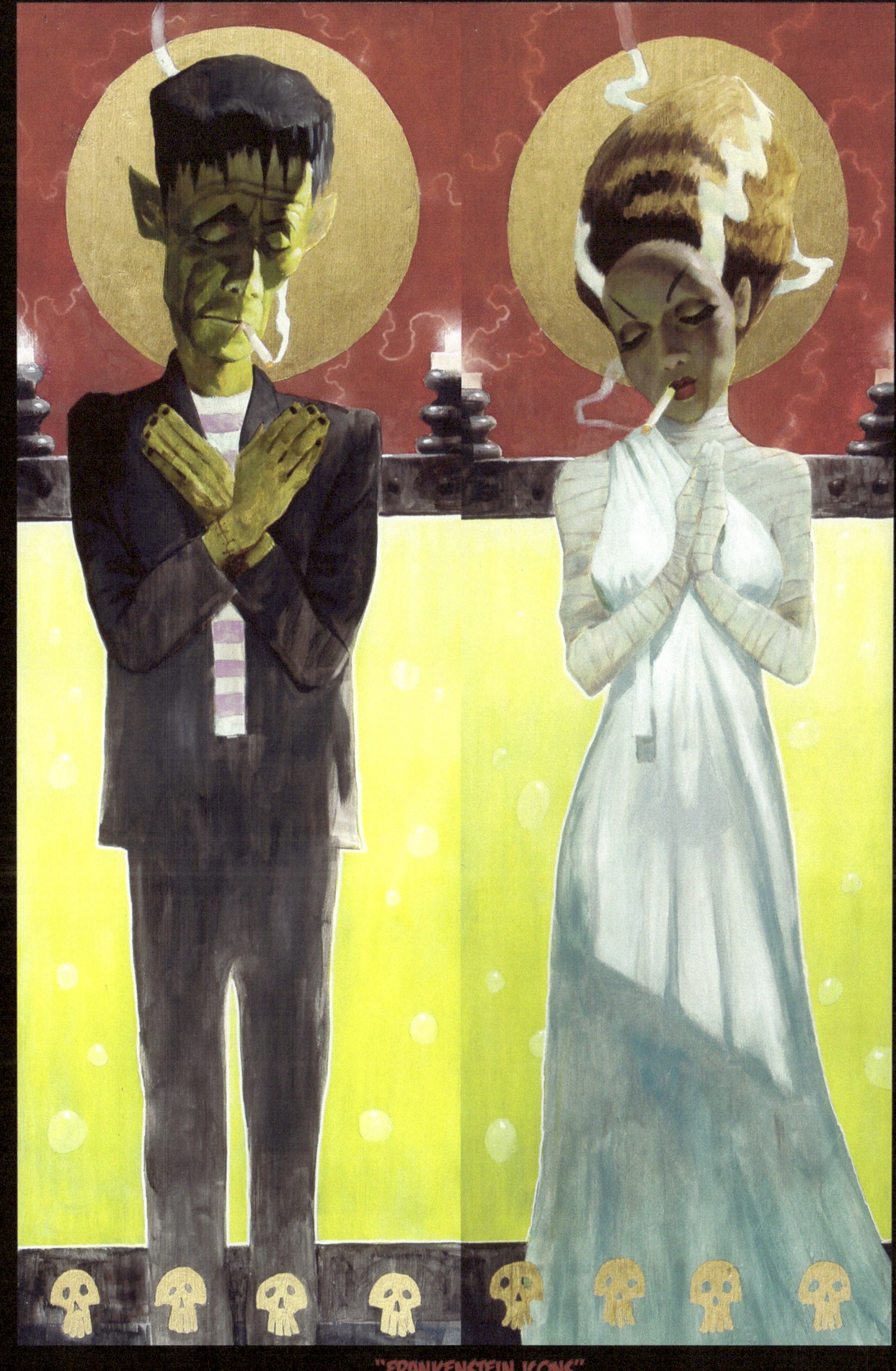

"FRANKENSTEIN ICONS"

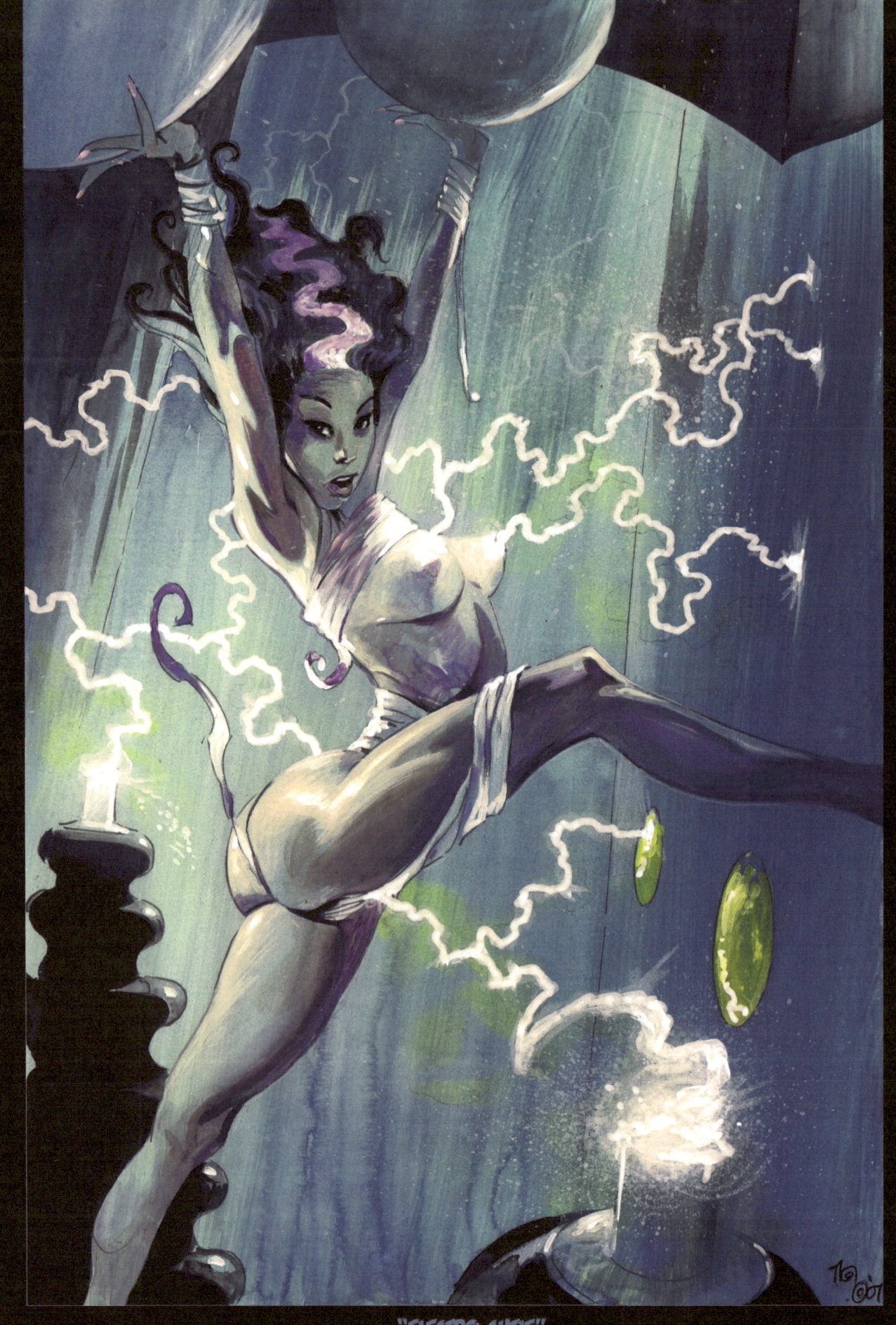

"ELECTRO-CUTIE"

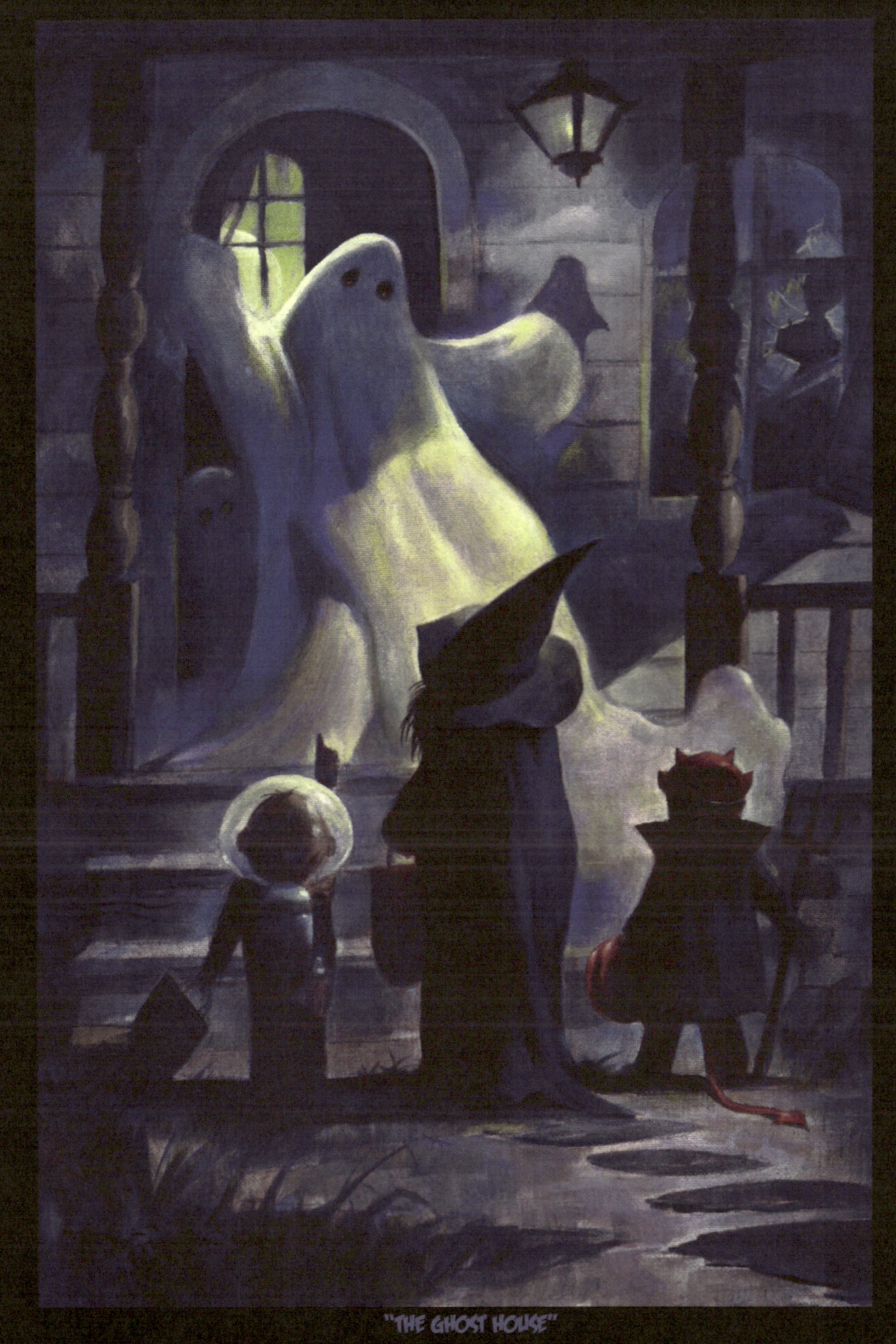

"THE GHOST HOUSE"

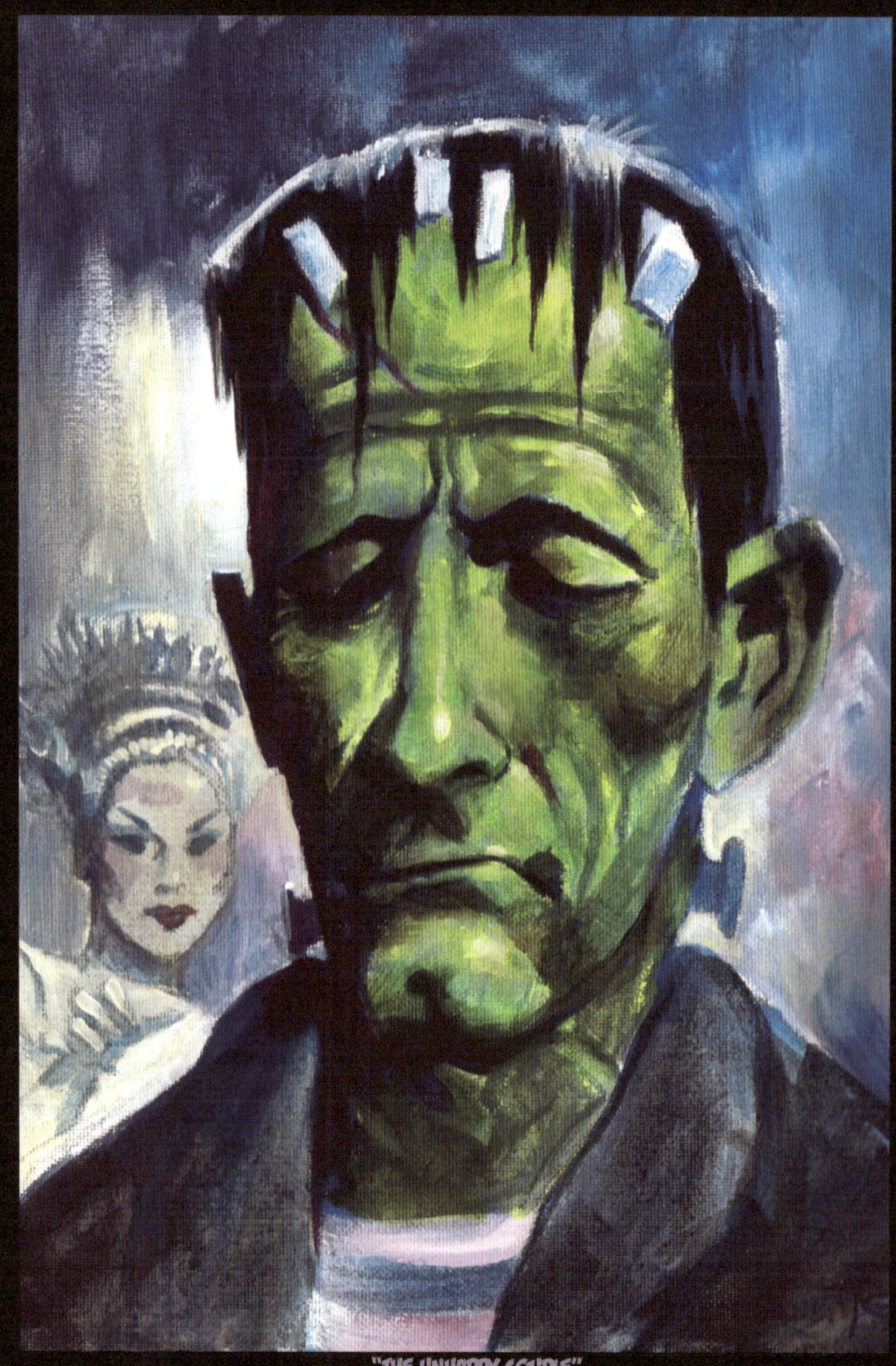

"THE UNHAPPY COUPLE"

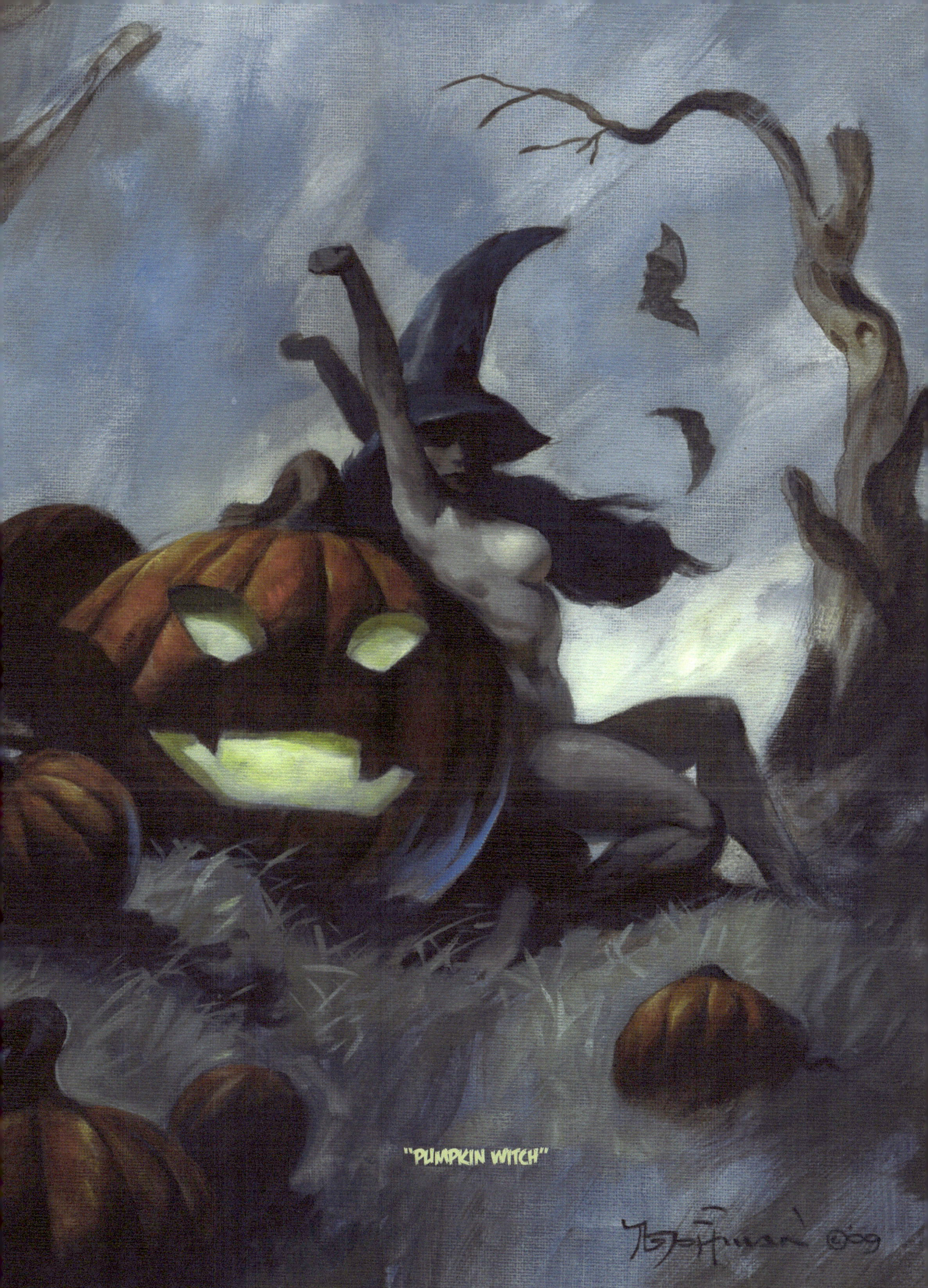

"PUMPKIN WITCH"

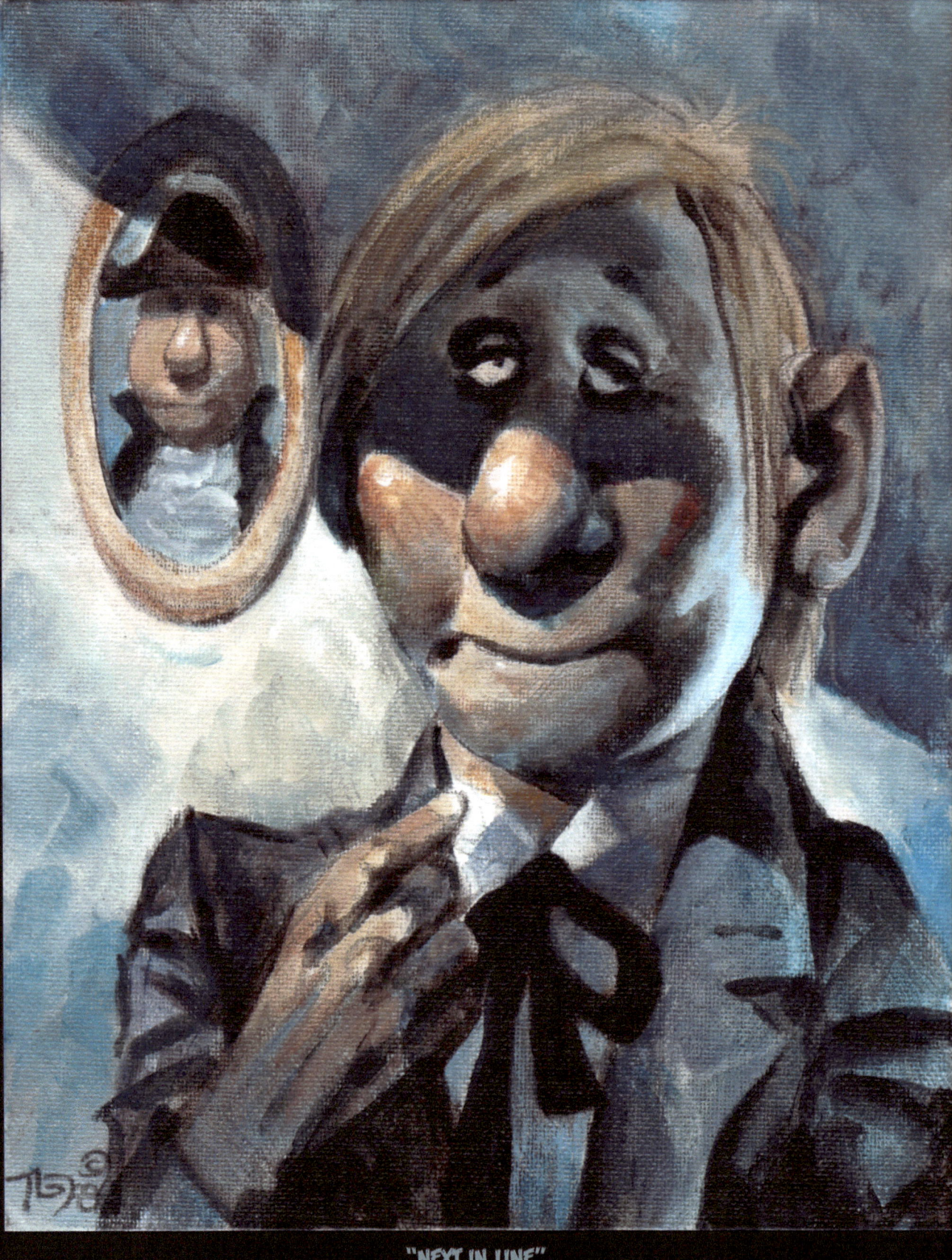

"NEXT IN LINE"

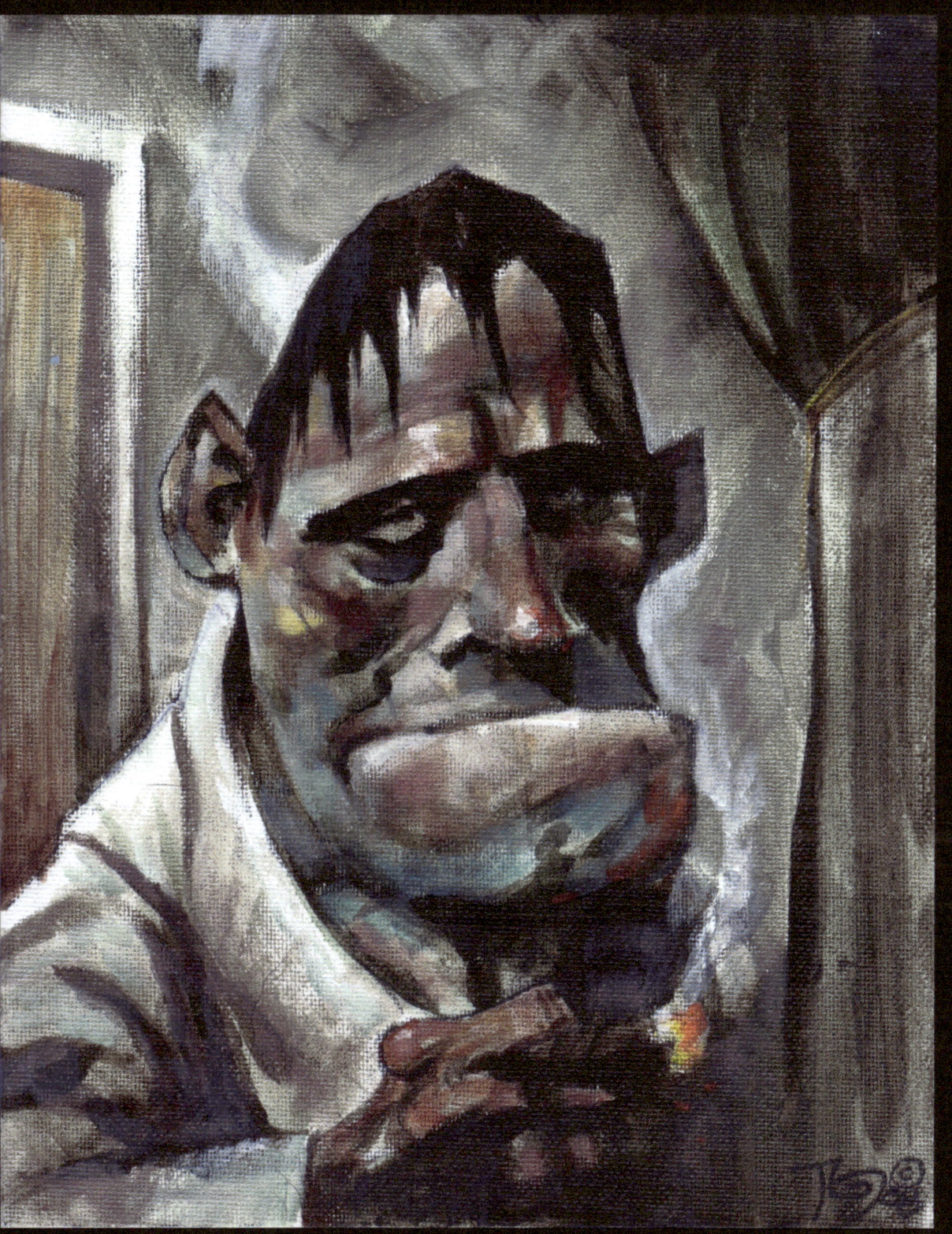

"YER OLD MAN"

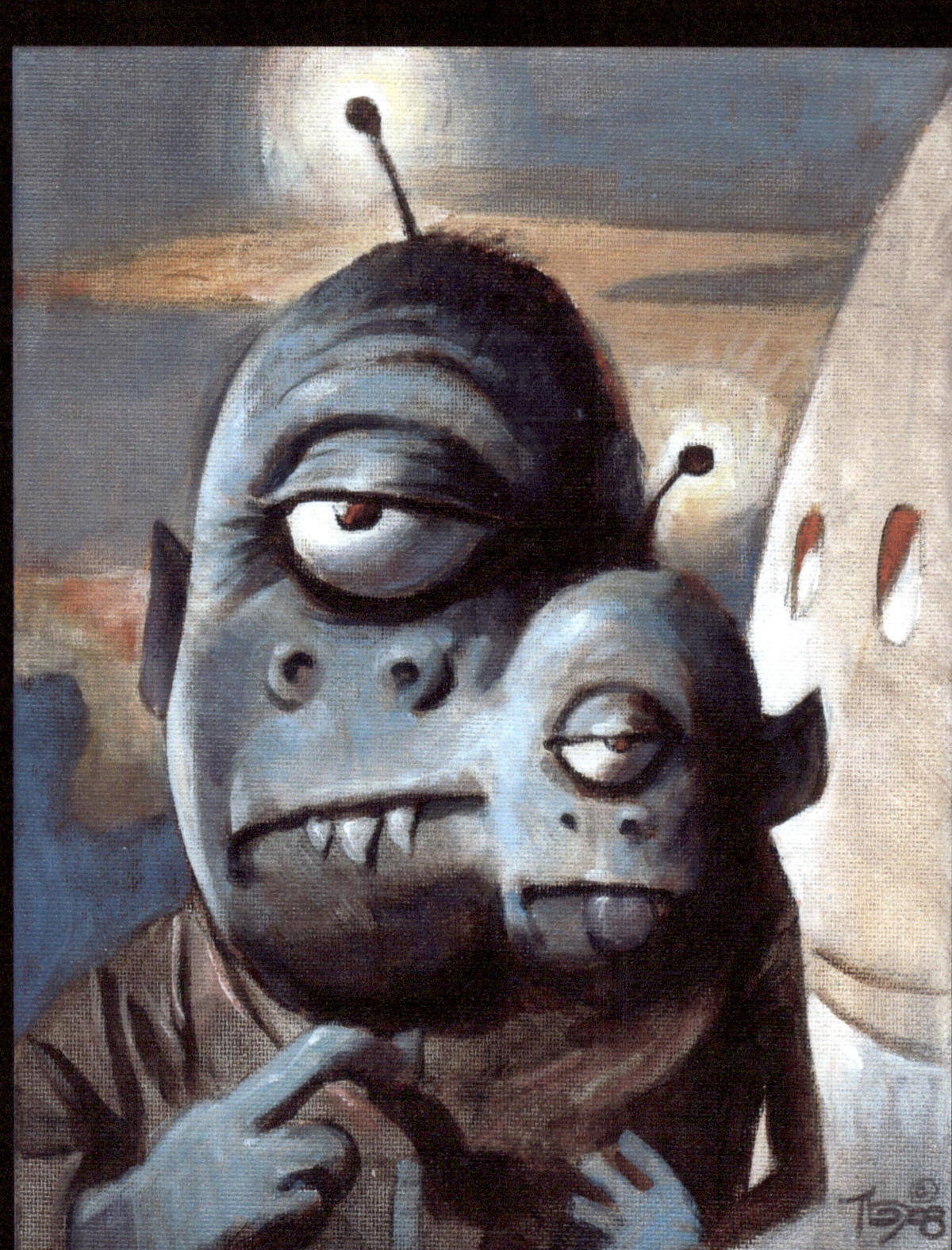

"UNINVITED GUESTS"

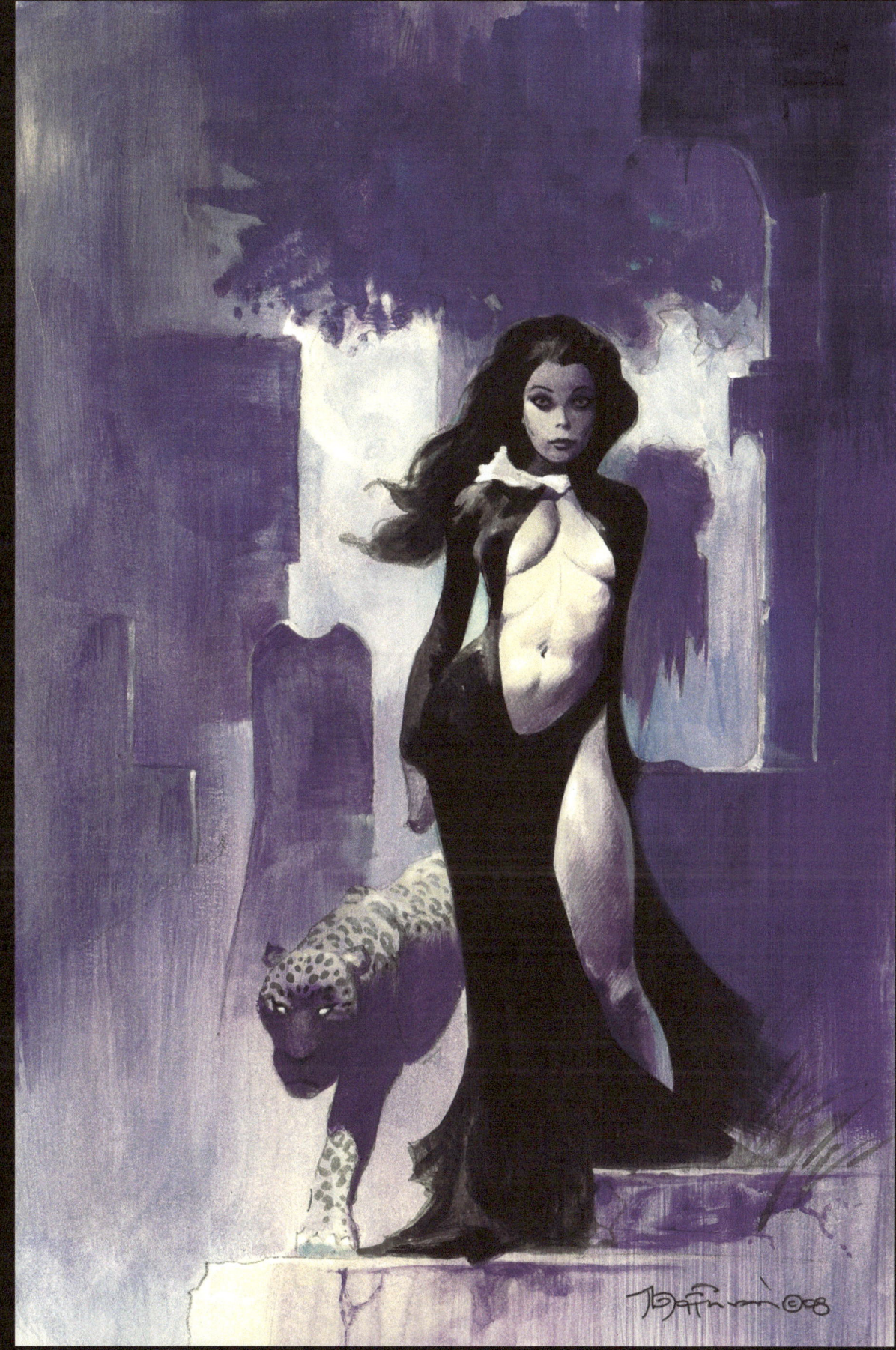

"CARMILLA STEELE"

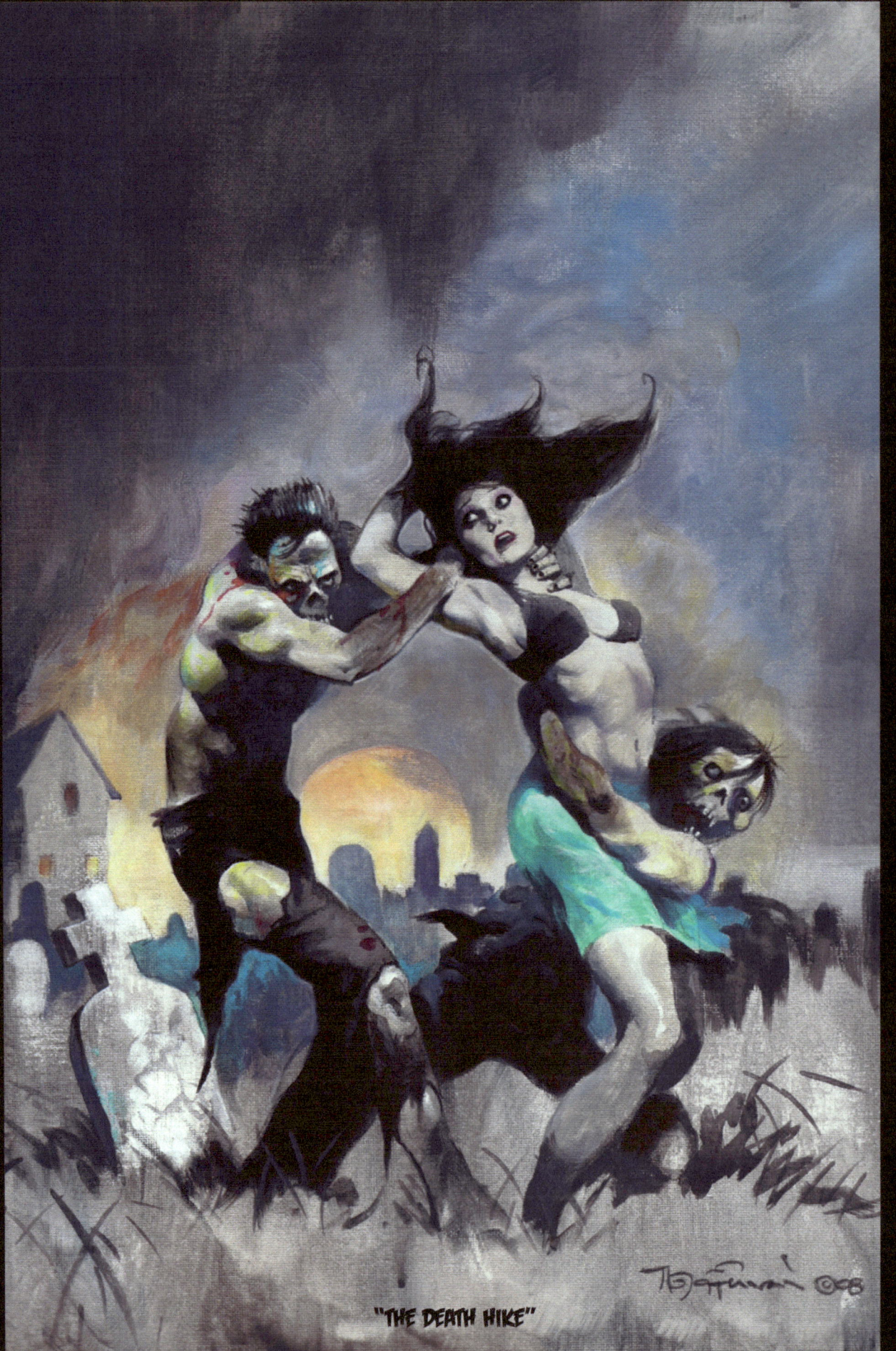

"THE DEATH HIKE"

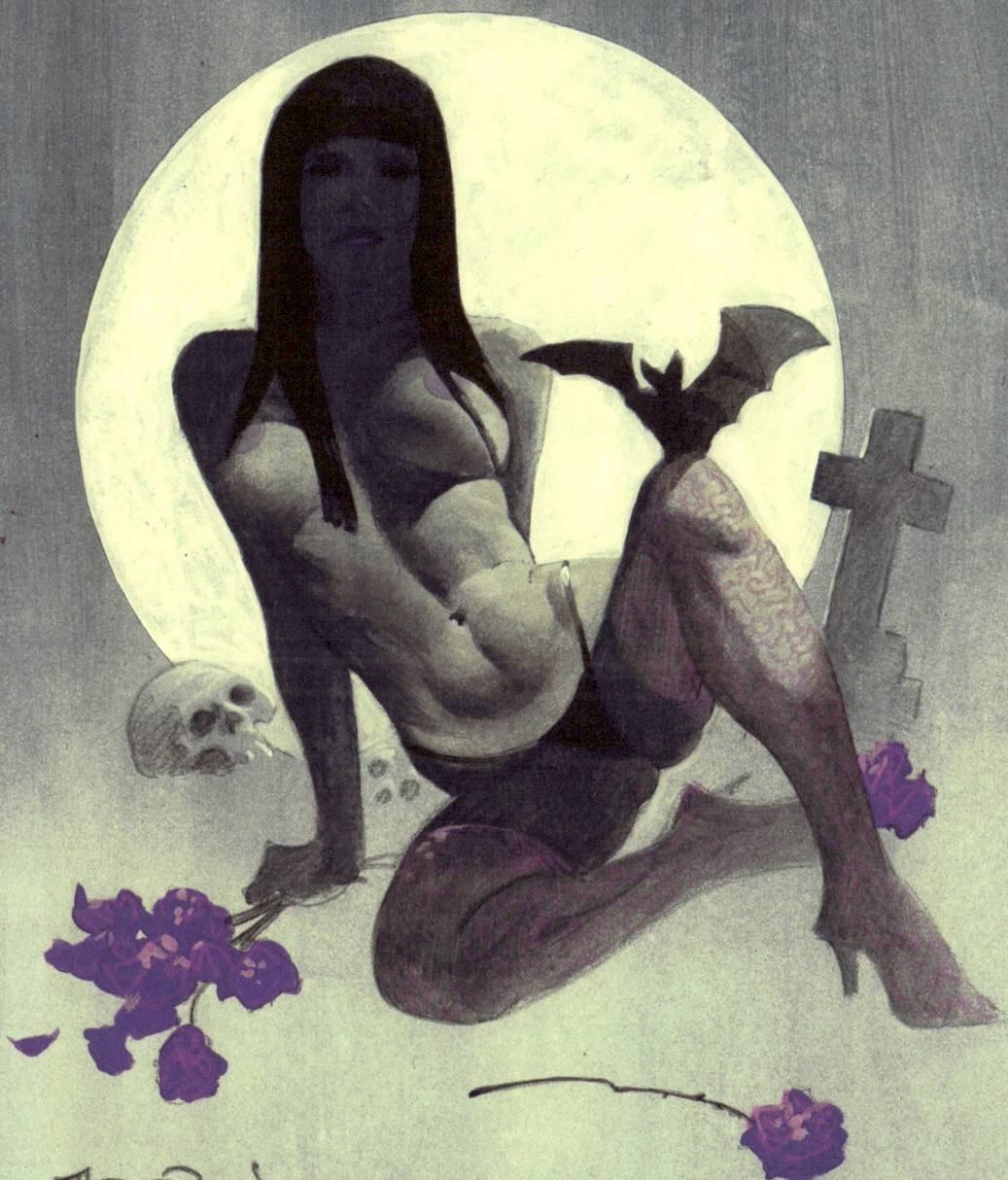

"DEADLY NIGHTSHADE"

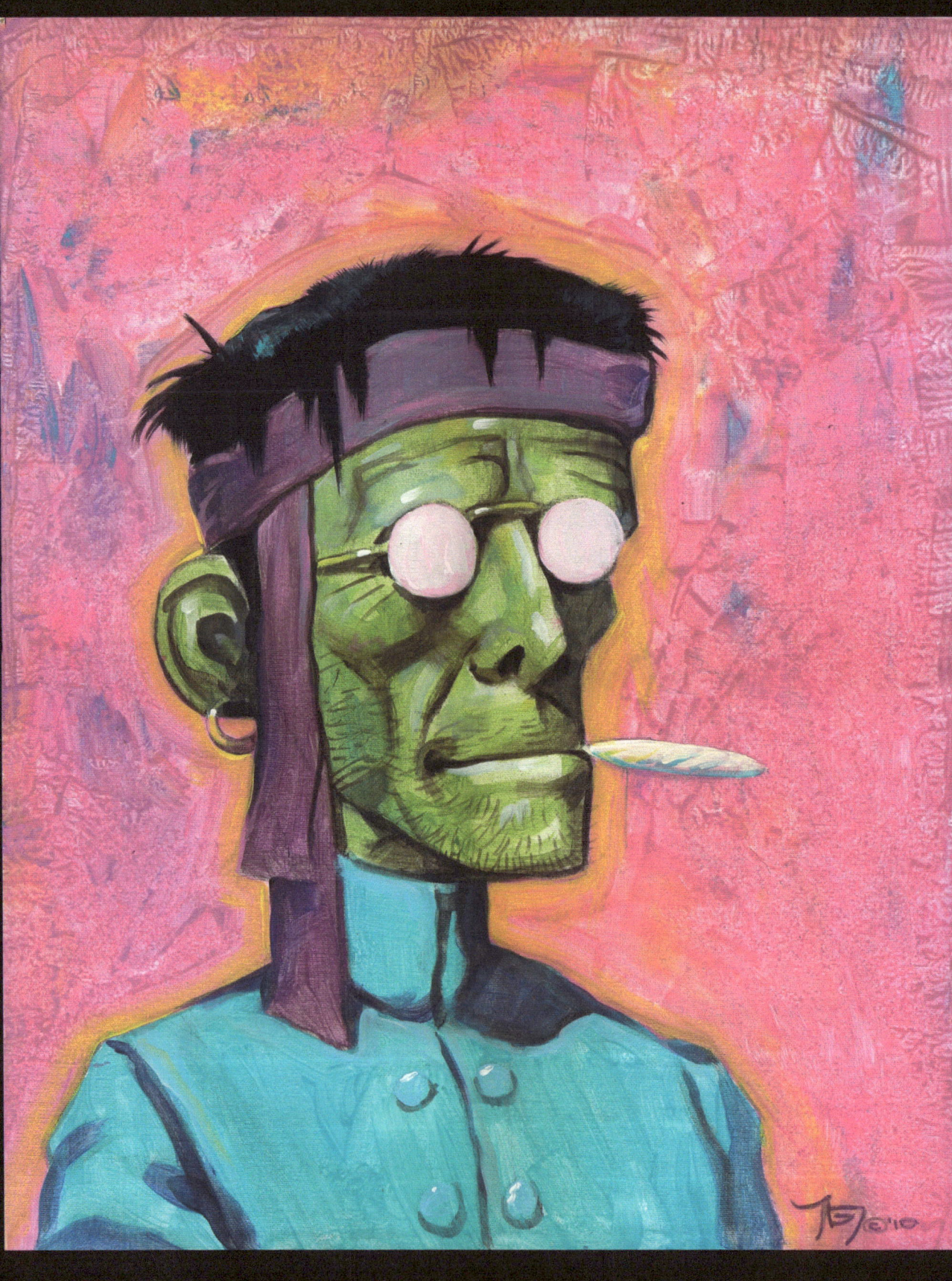

"HIPPIE FRANKENSTEIN"

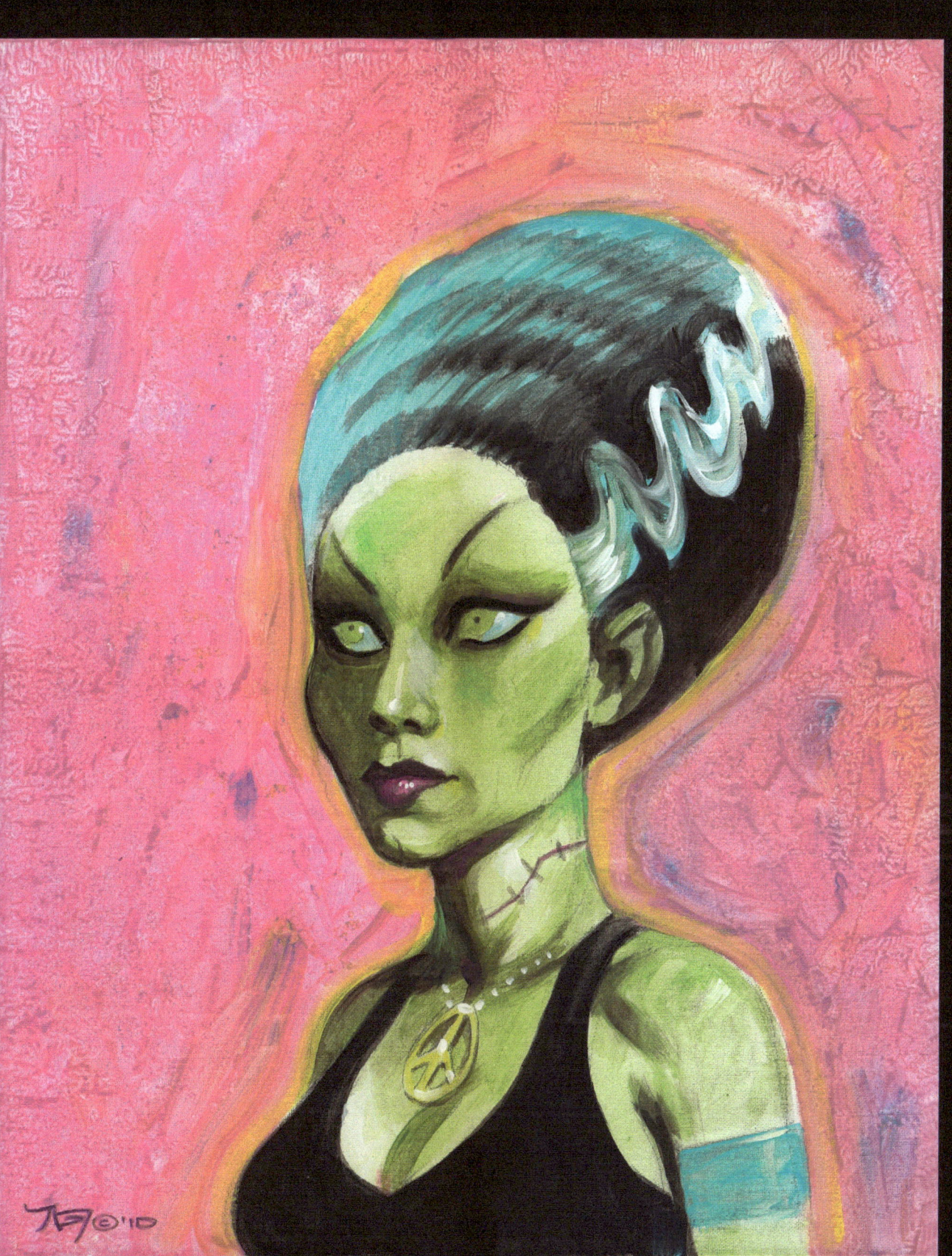

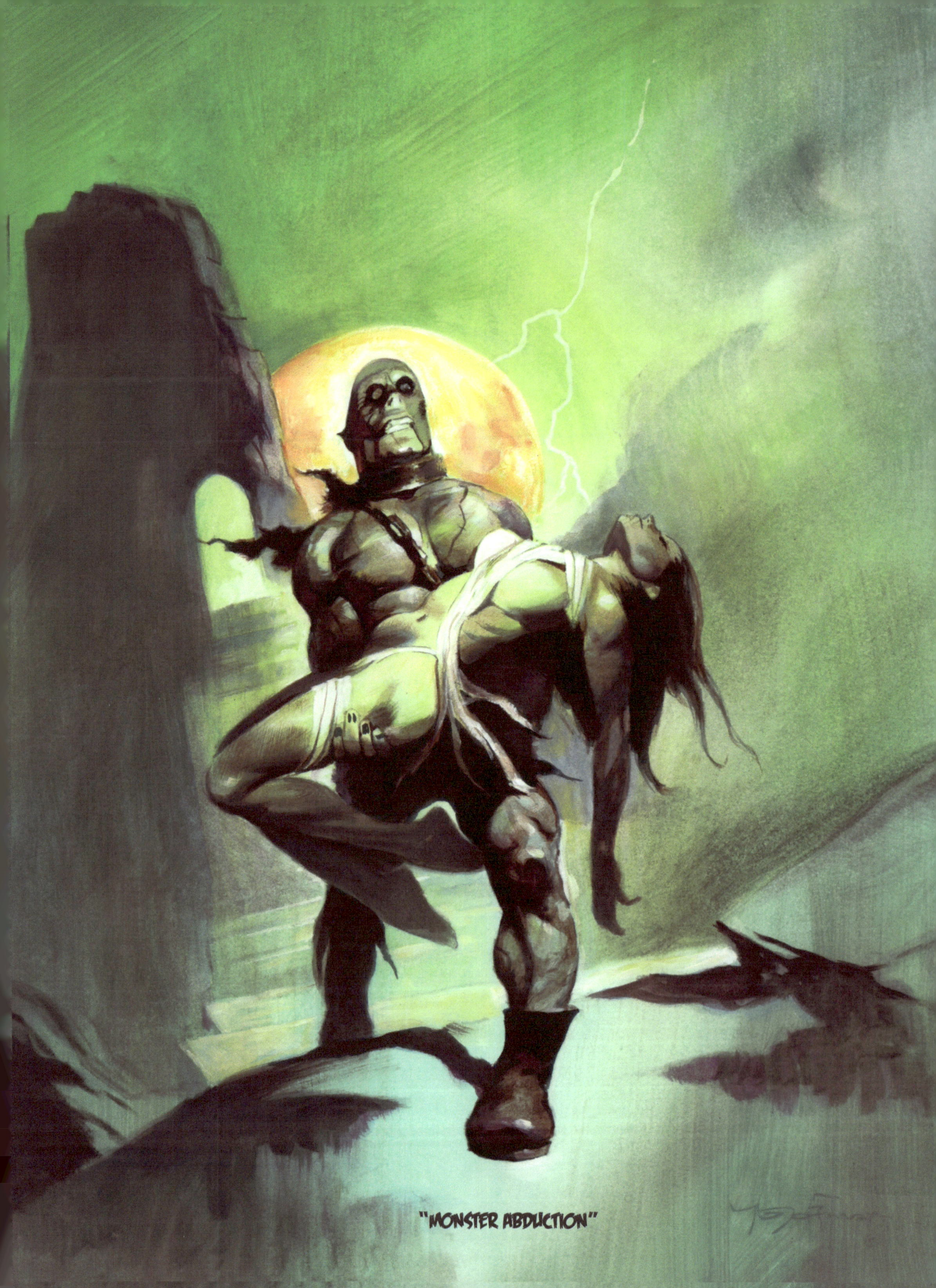

"MONSTER ABDUCTION"

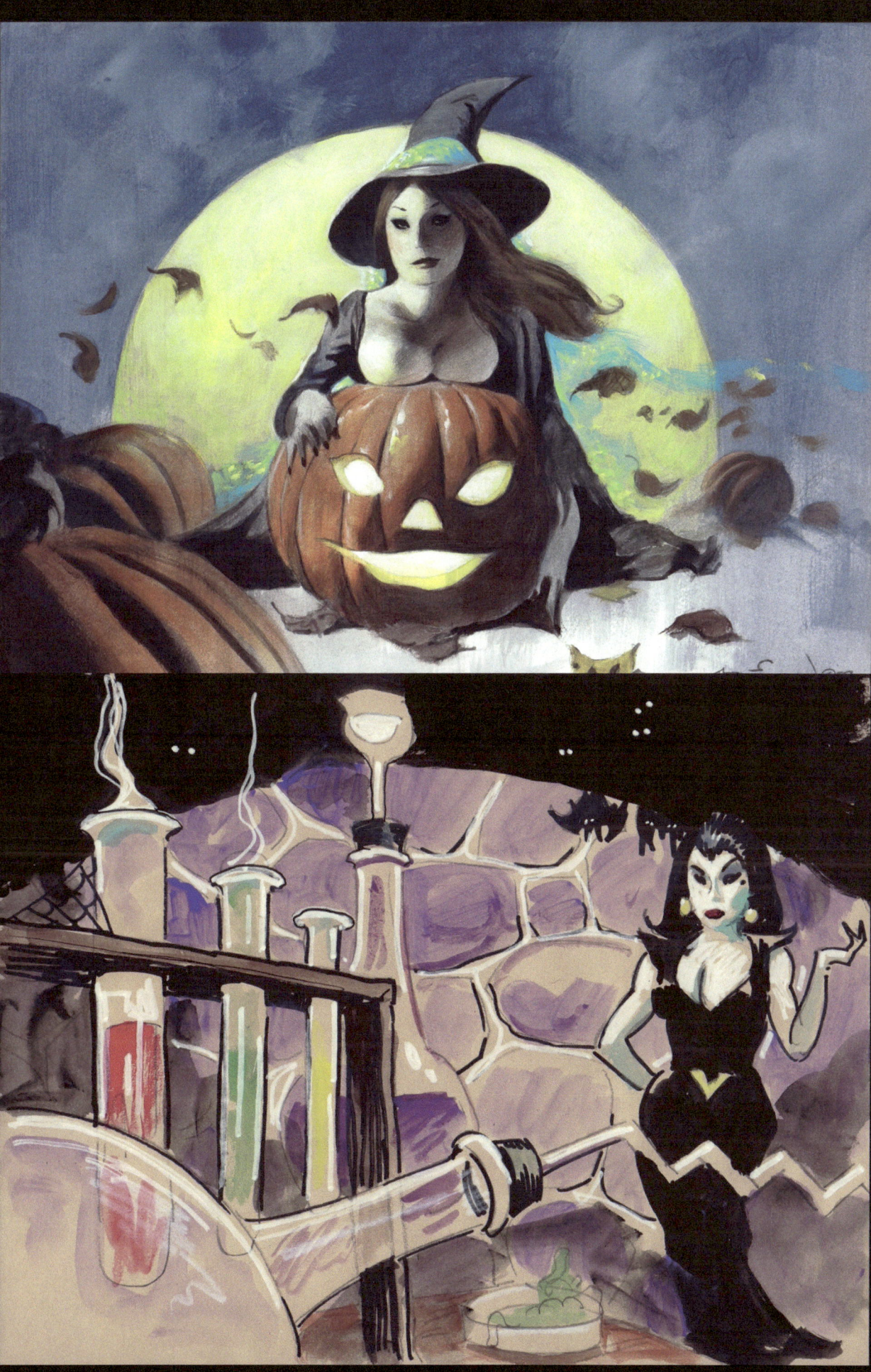

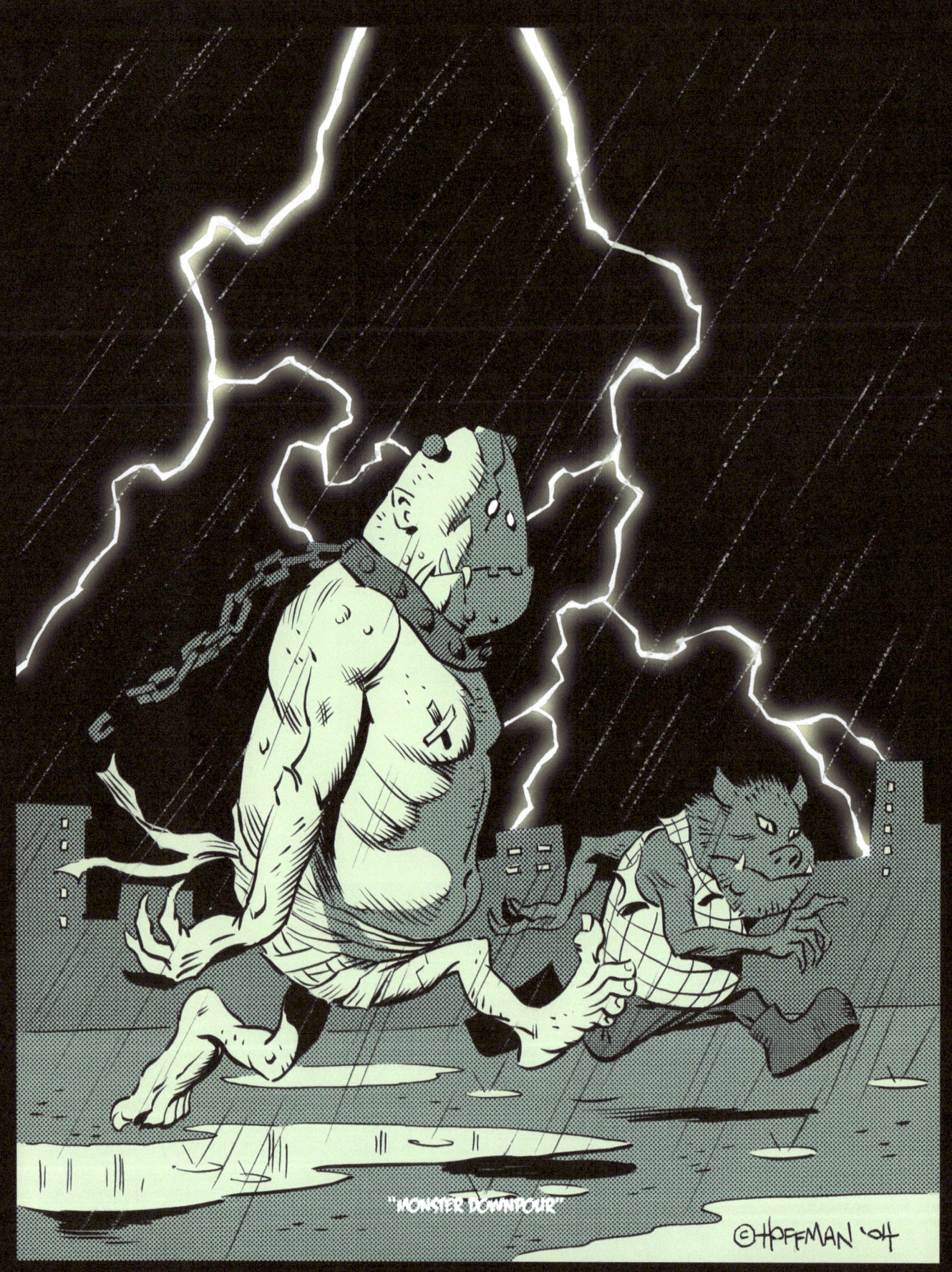

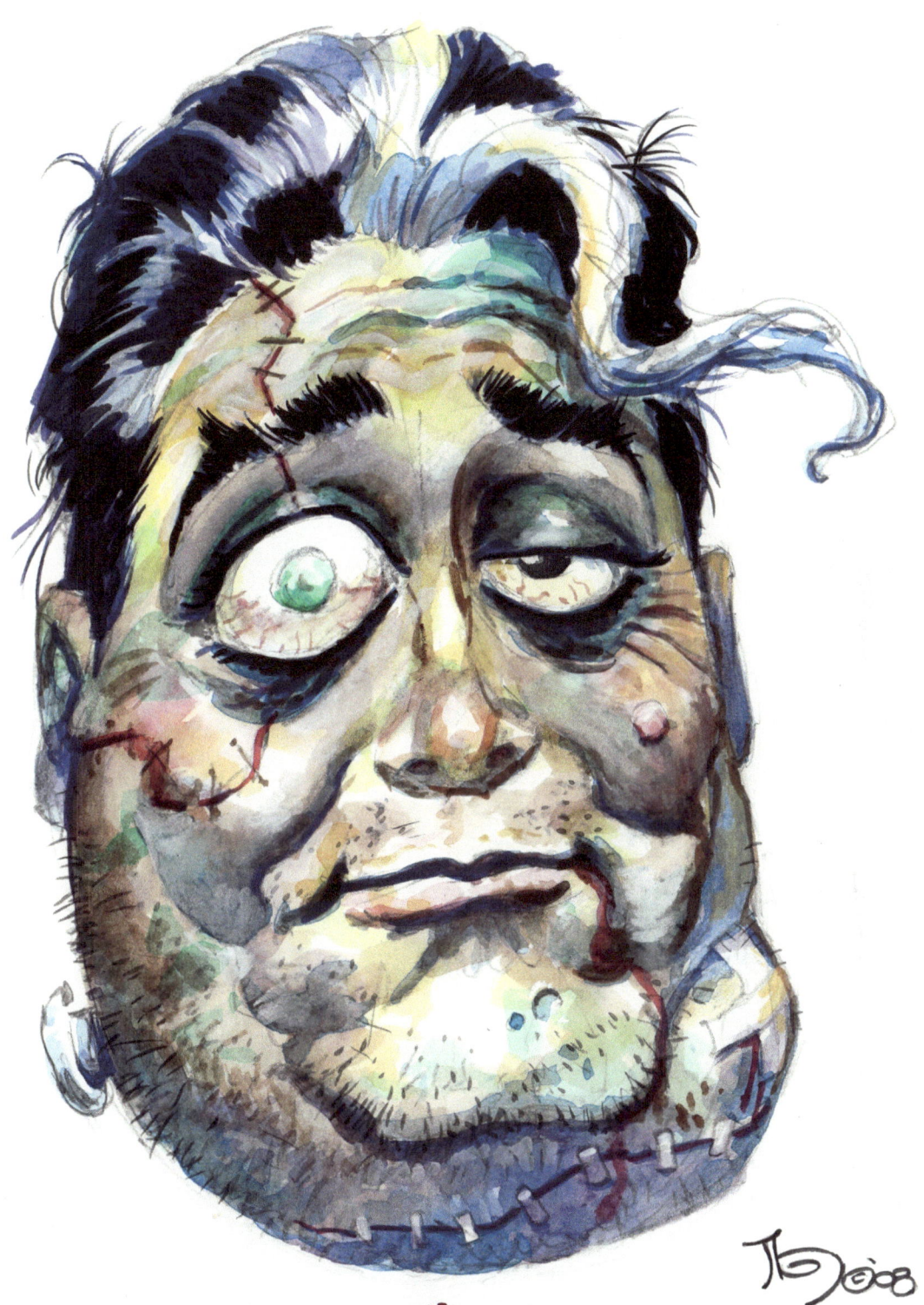

JERKIE GRUESOME

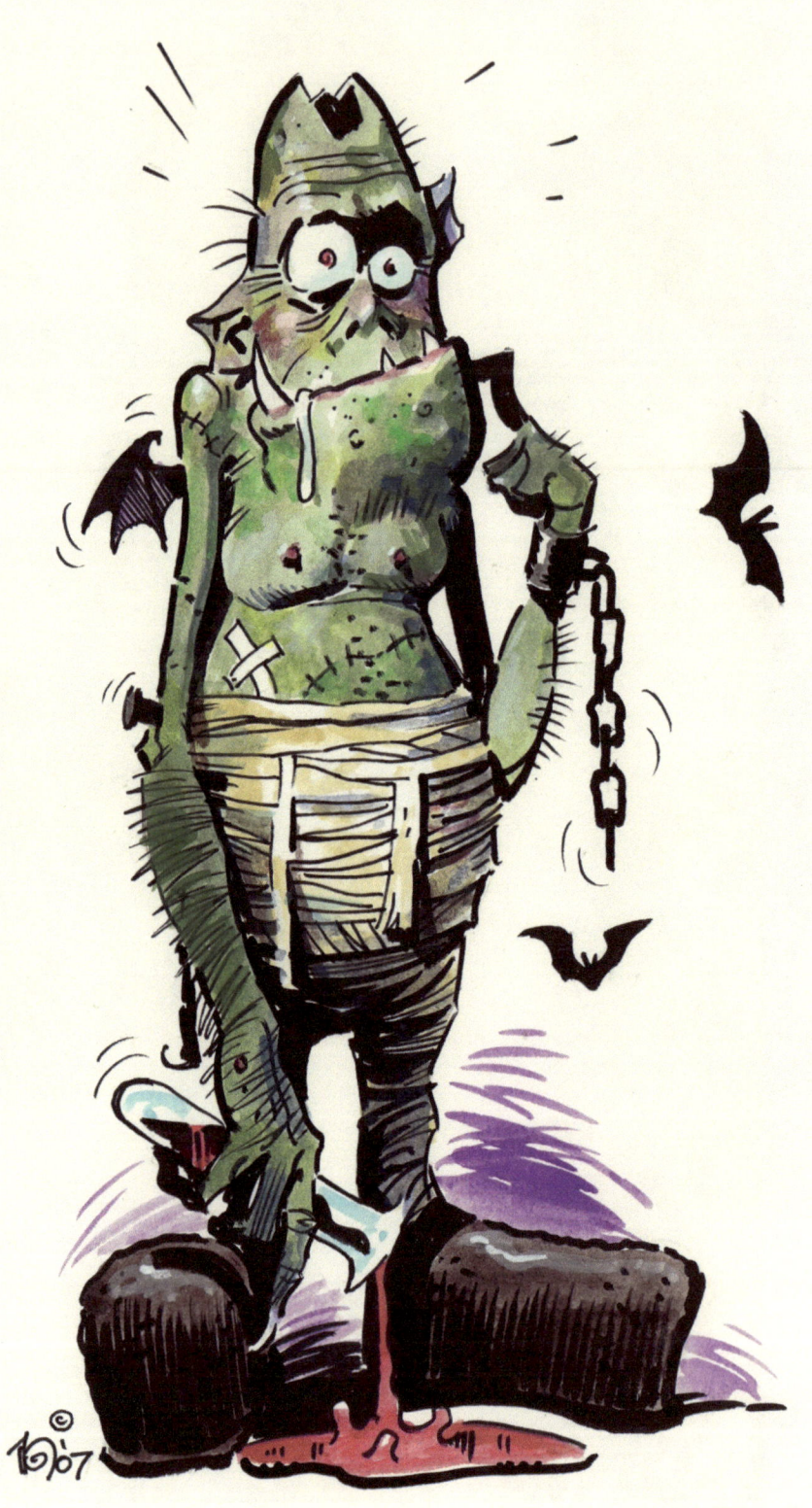

"IT ONLY HURTS..."

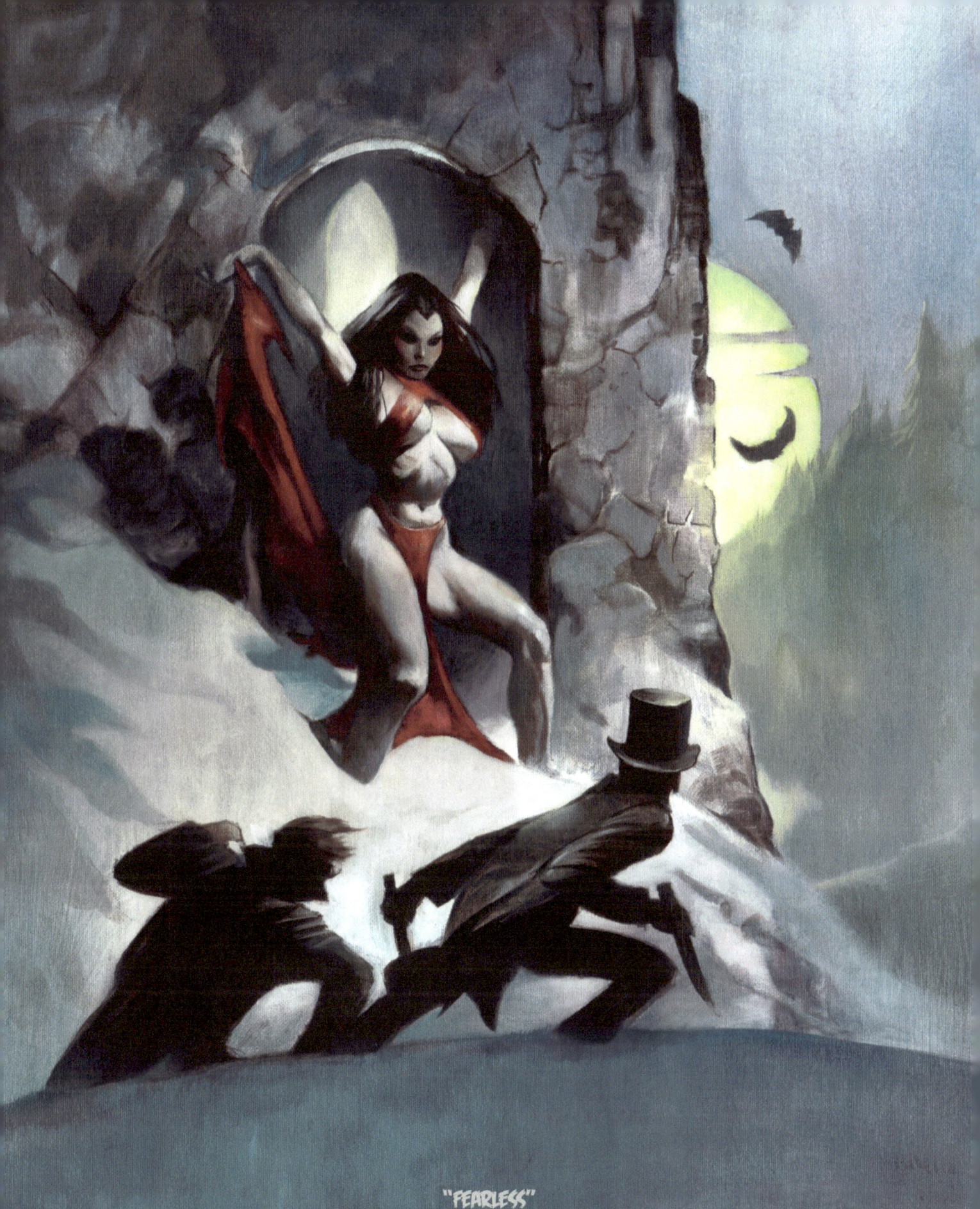

"FEARLESS"

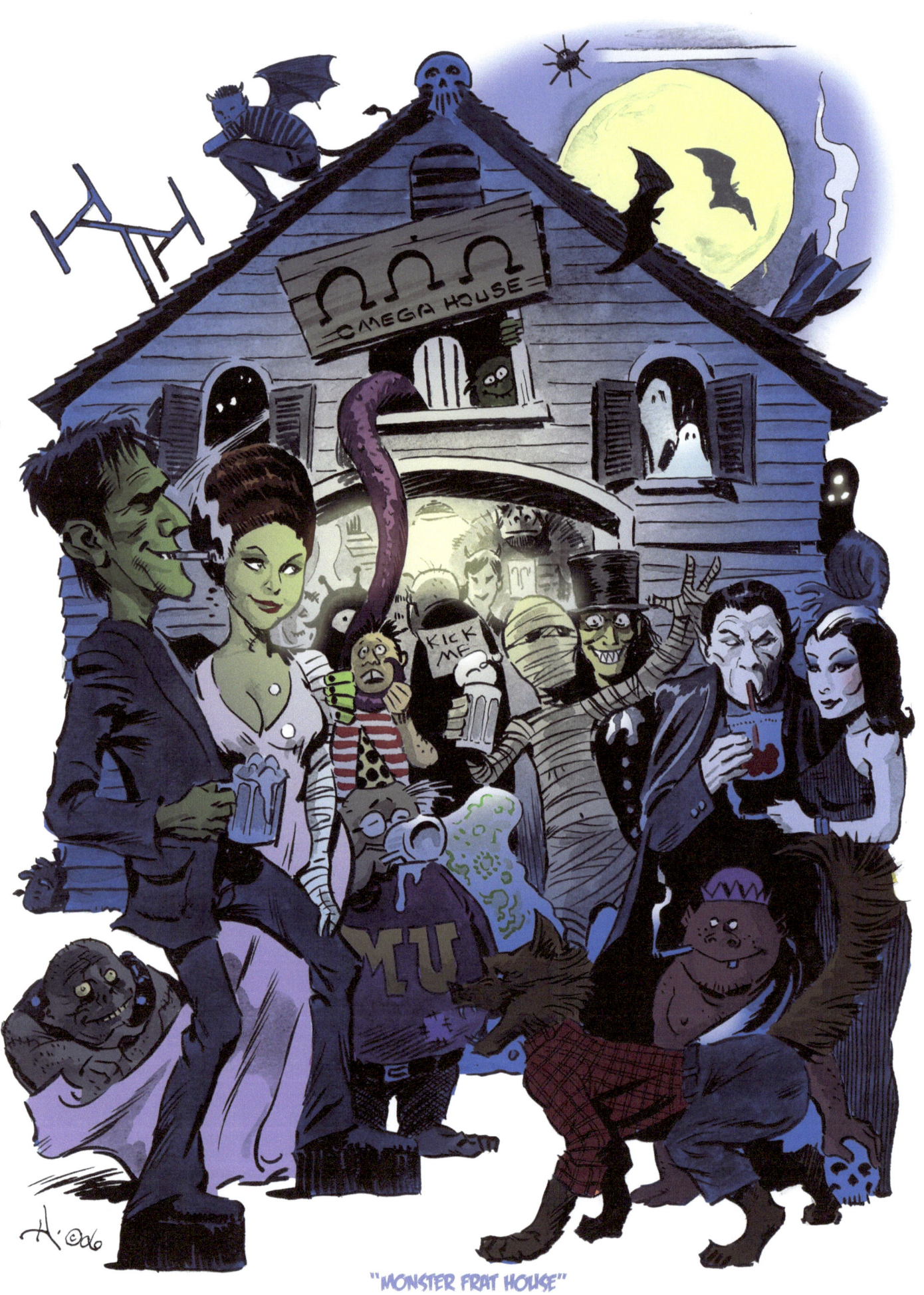

"MONSTER FRAT HOUSE"

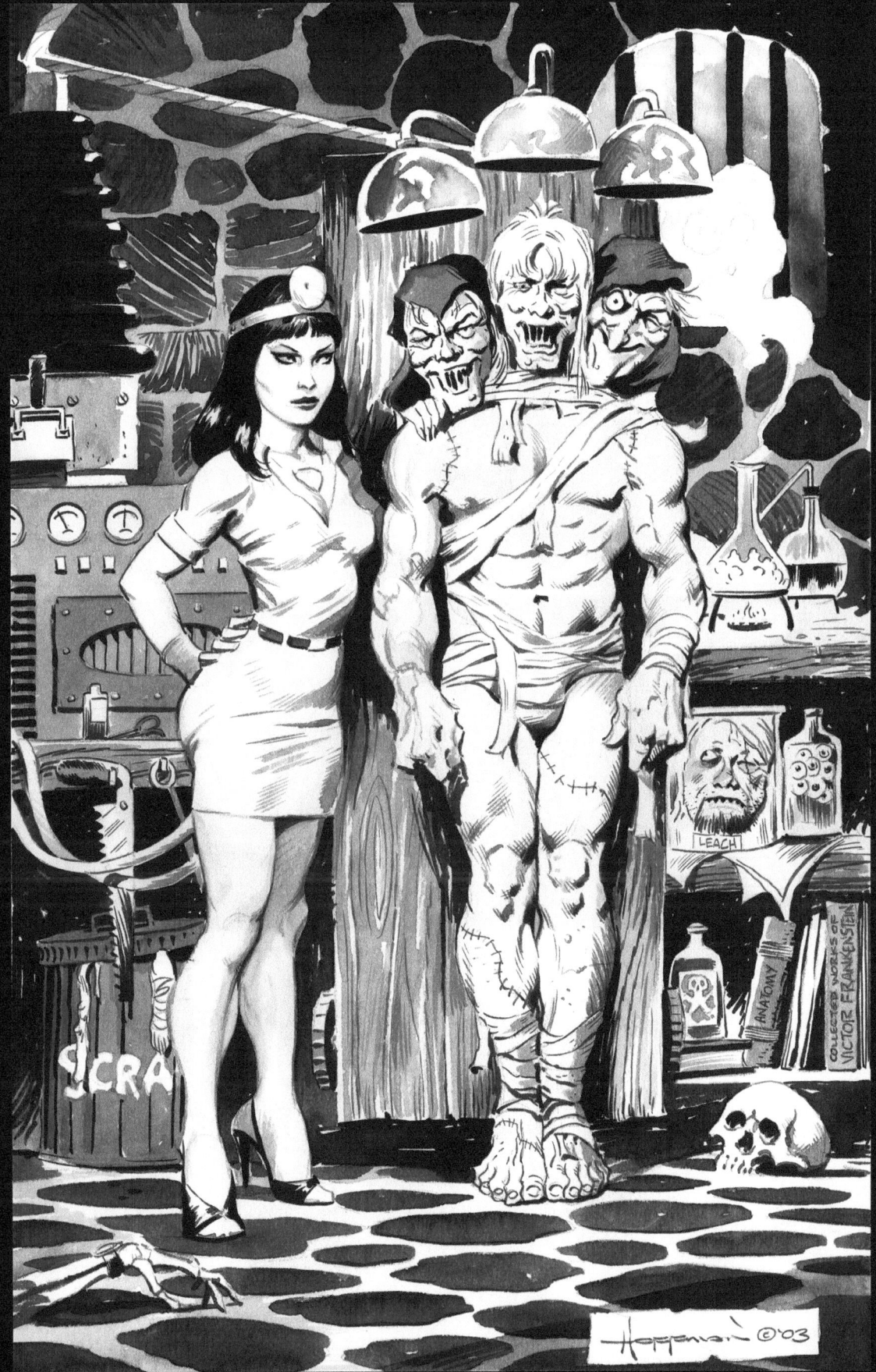

"THE GHOULUNATICS"

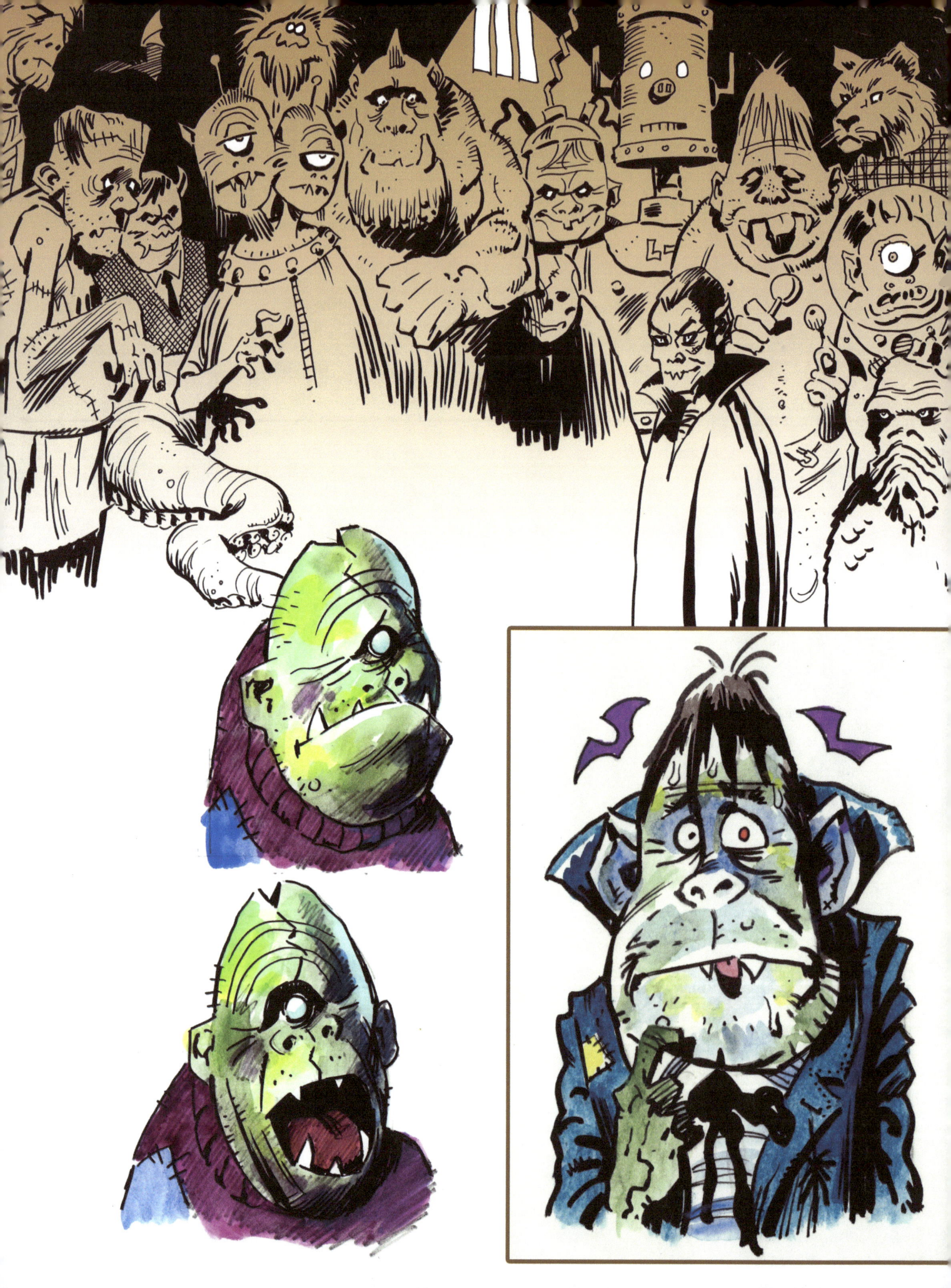

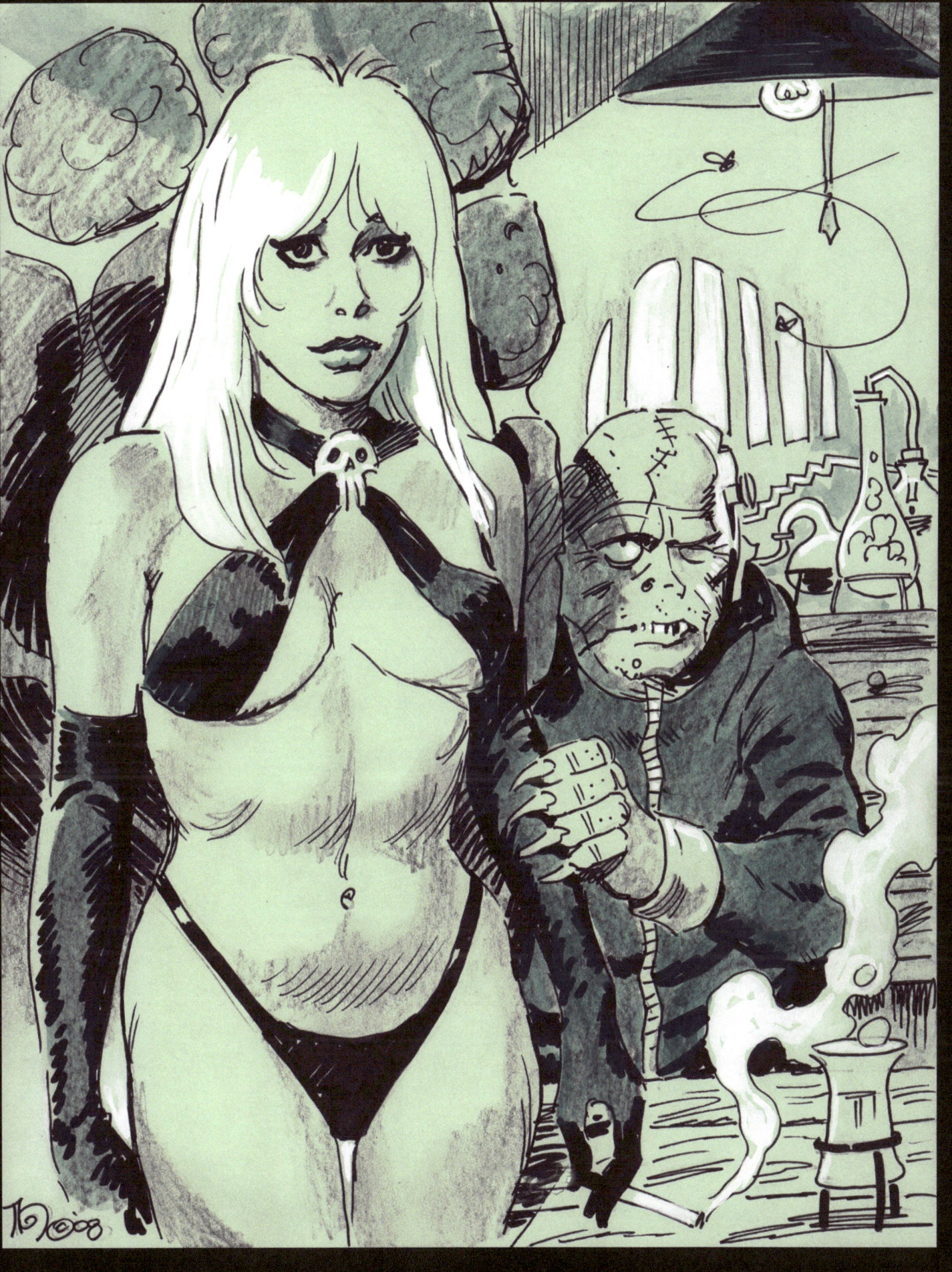

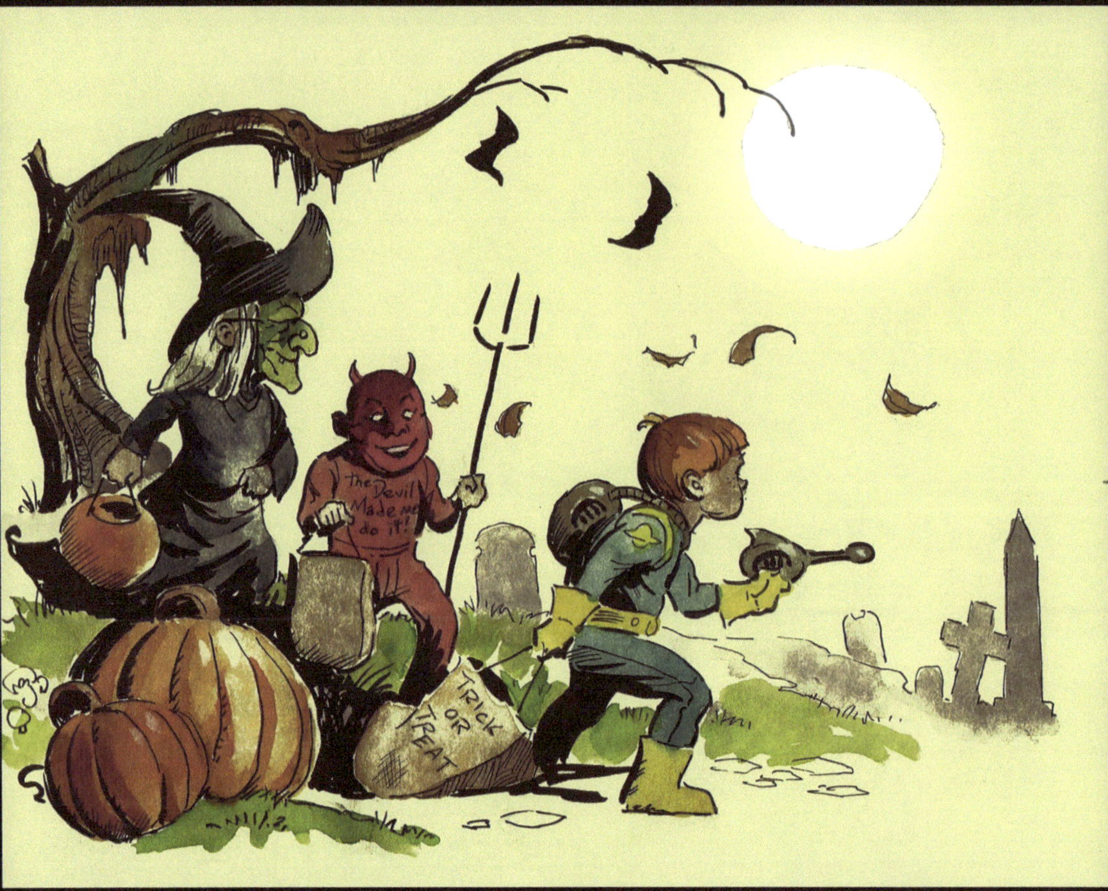
The Devil Made me do it!
TRICK OR TREAT

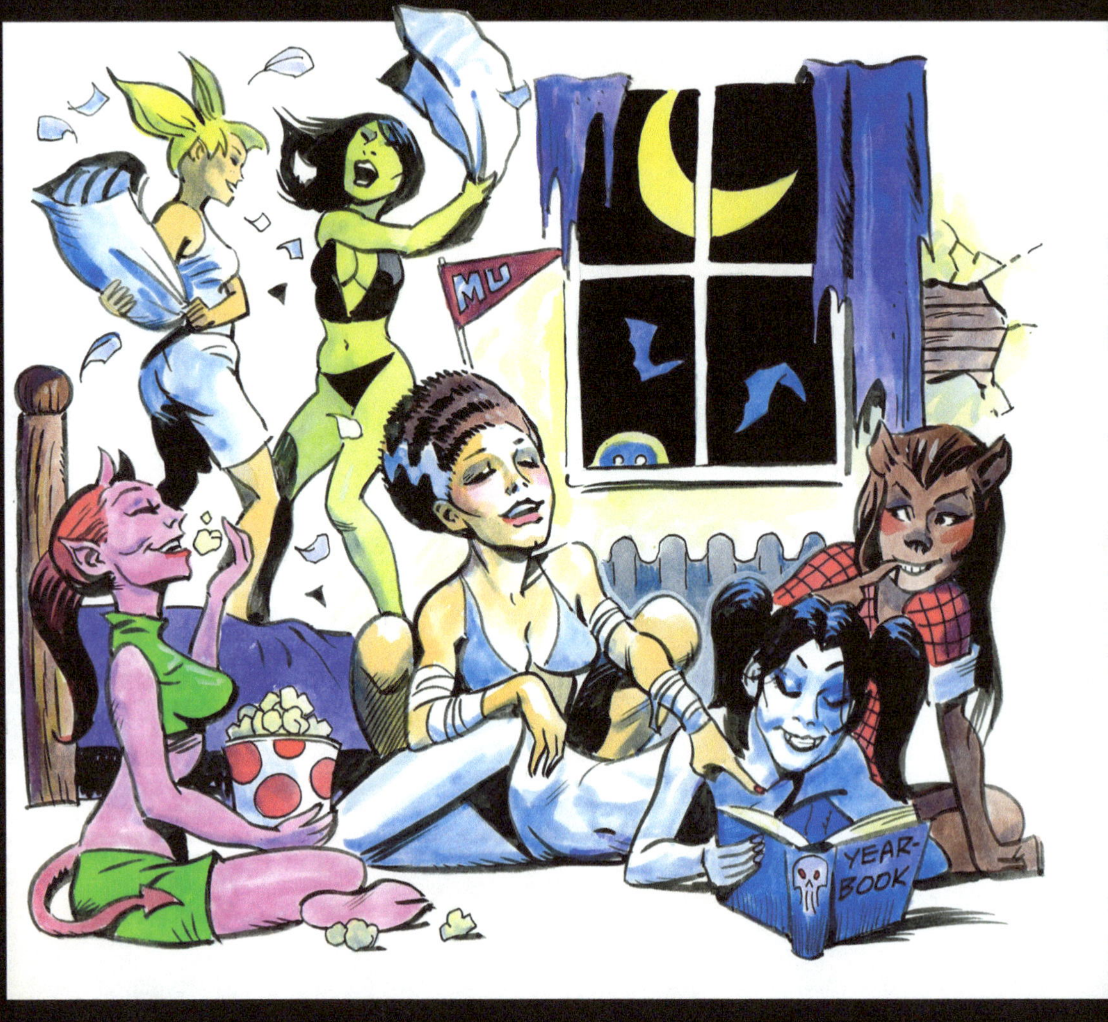
MU
YEAR-BOOK

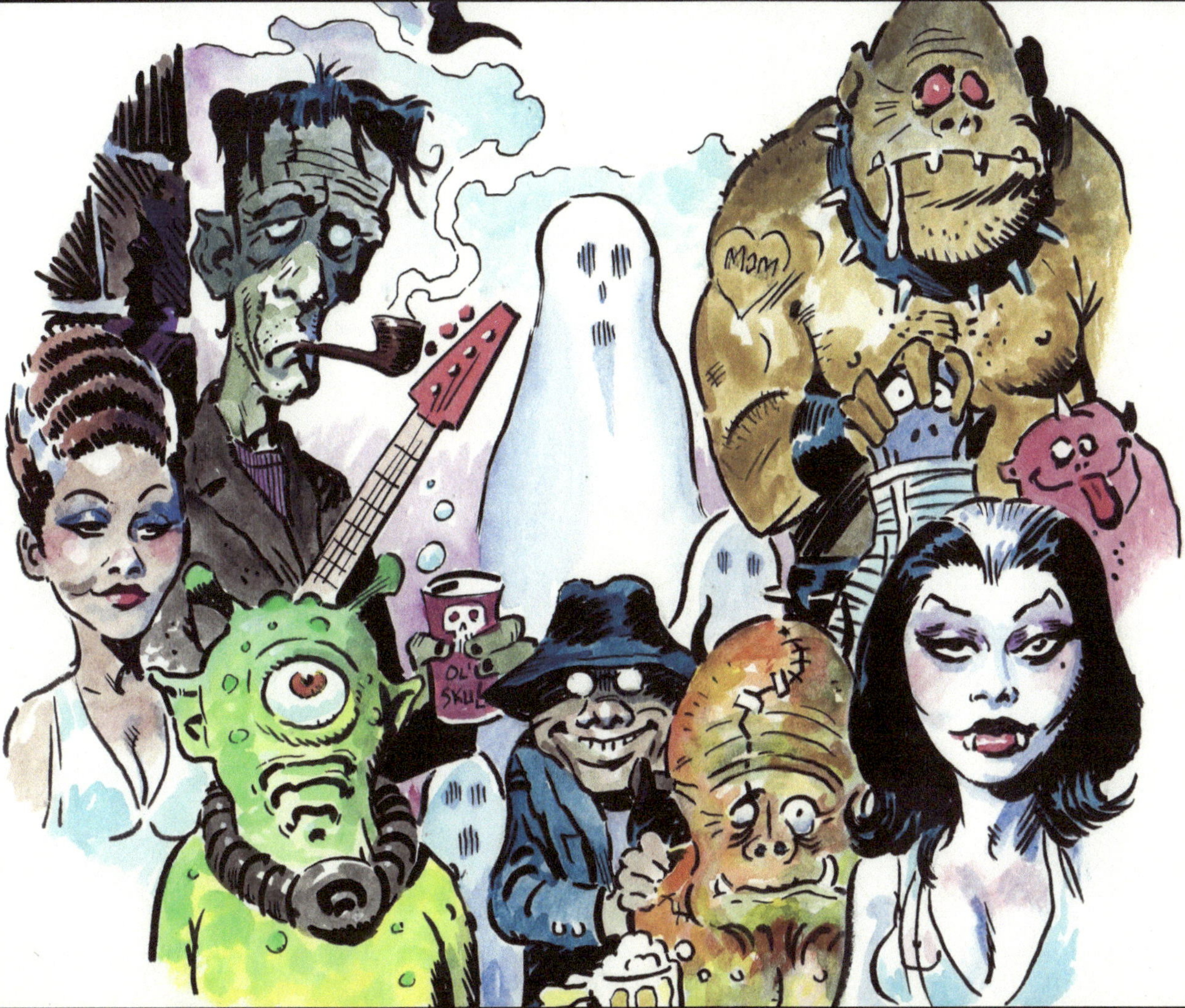
Mom

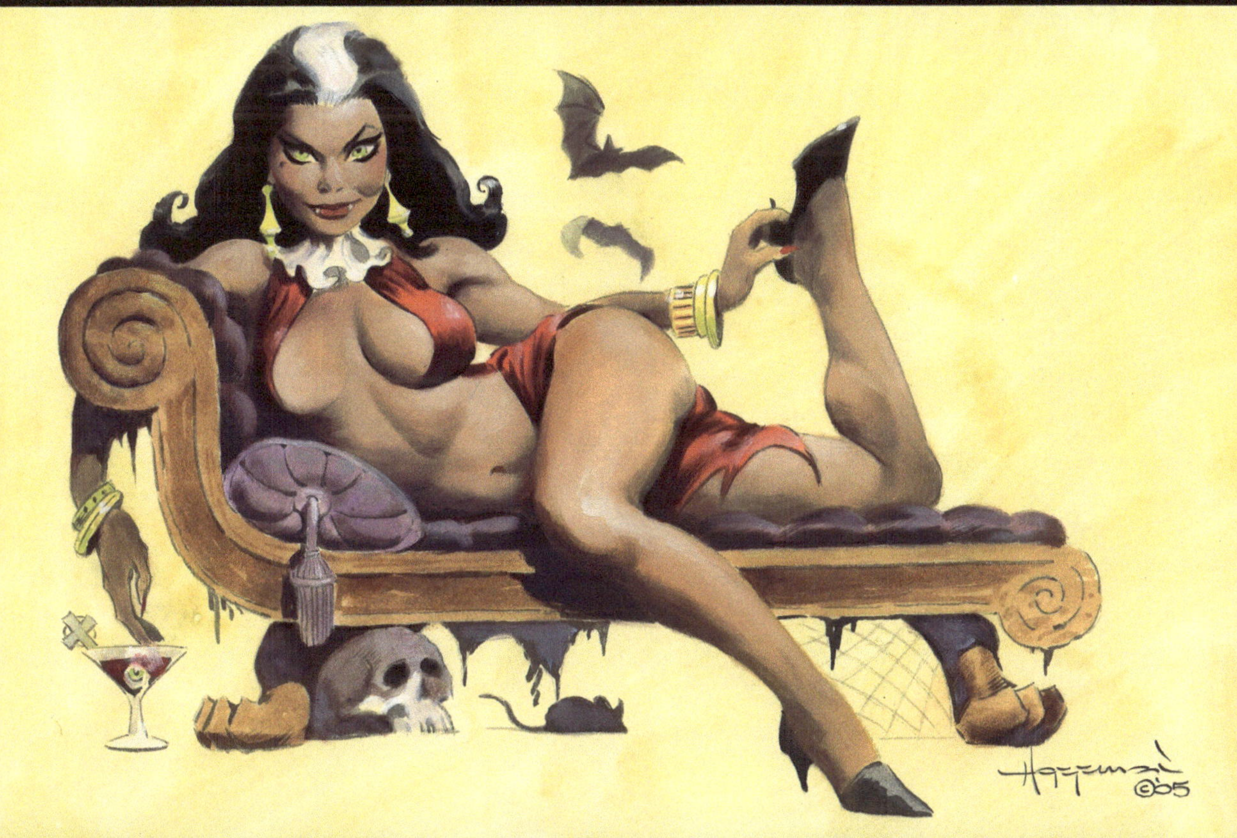

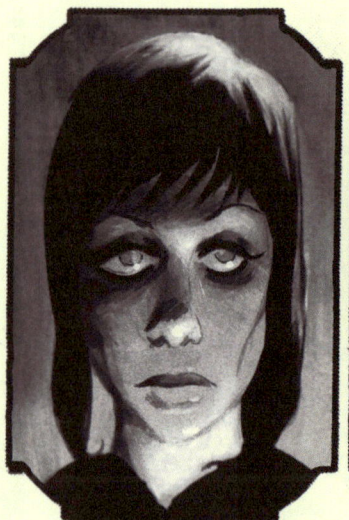

Onyx Dulux
Drama, Embalming Club

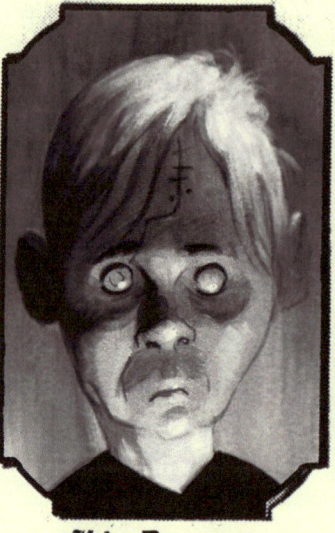

Kid Daverson
Poisoning 101

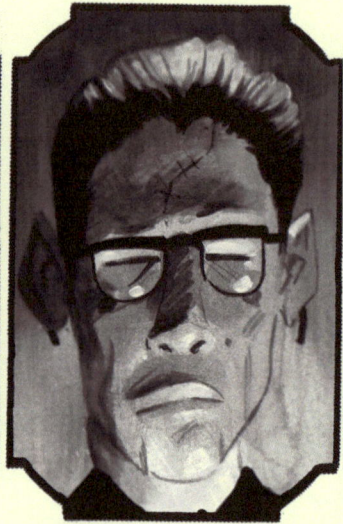

Rusty Tetanus
Transmutation Club, Lab

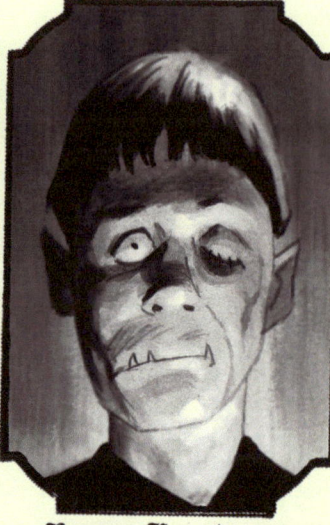

Larry Fanghurst
Advanced Bloodletting

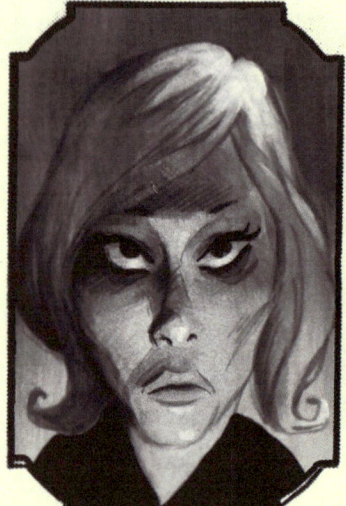

Elenora Gunch
Future Tombmakers

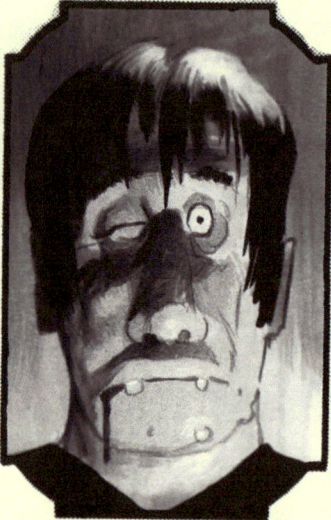

Orville Moonbeem
Lycanthropy Squad

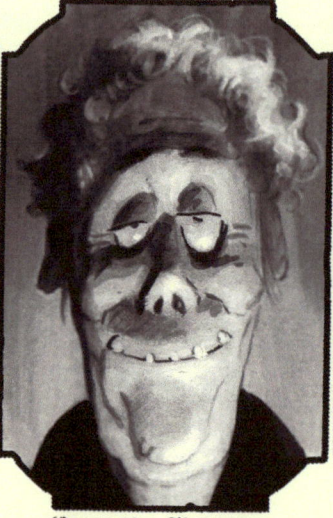

Oswald Haywar
Teacher Assistant

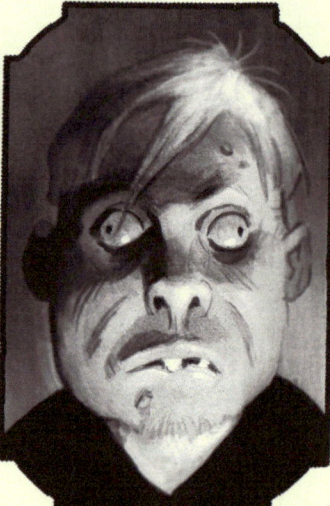

Wallace Eyesore
Archery, Girlwatchers Club

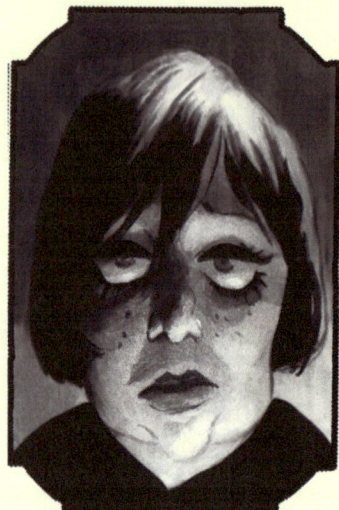

Nausea Von Bedpan
Unhealth Club, Civics

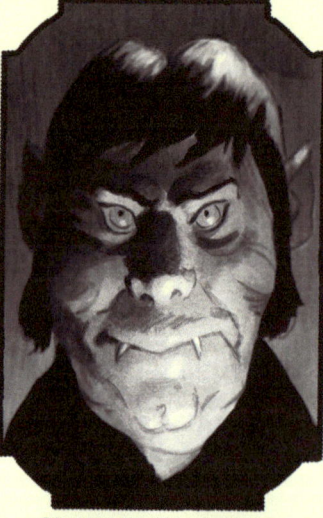

Norvile Stakehart
Night Class, Mixology

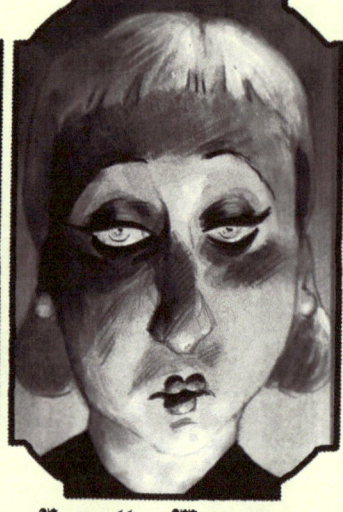

Prunella Westwing
Society Club, Bone Knitting

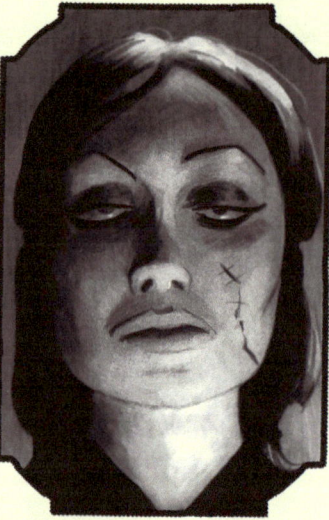

Clytemnestra Dutch
Necrology, Nymphomaniactics

"STUDENT BODY"

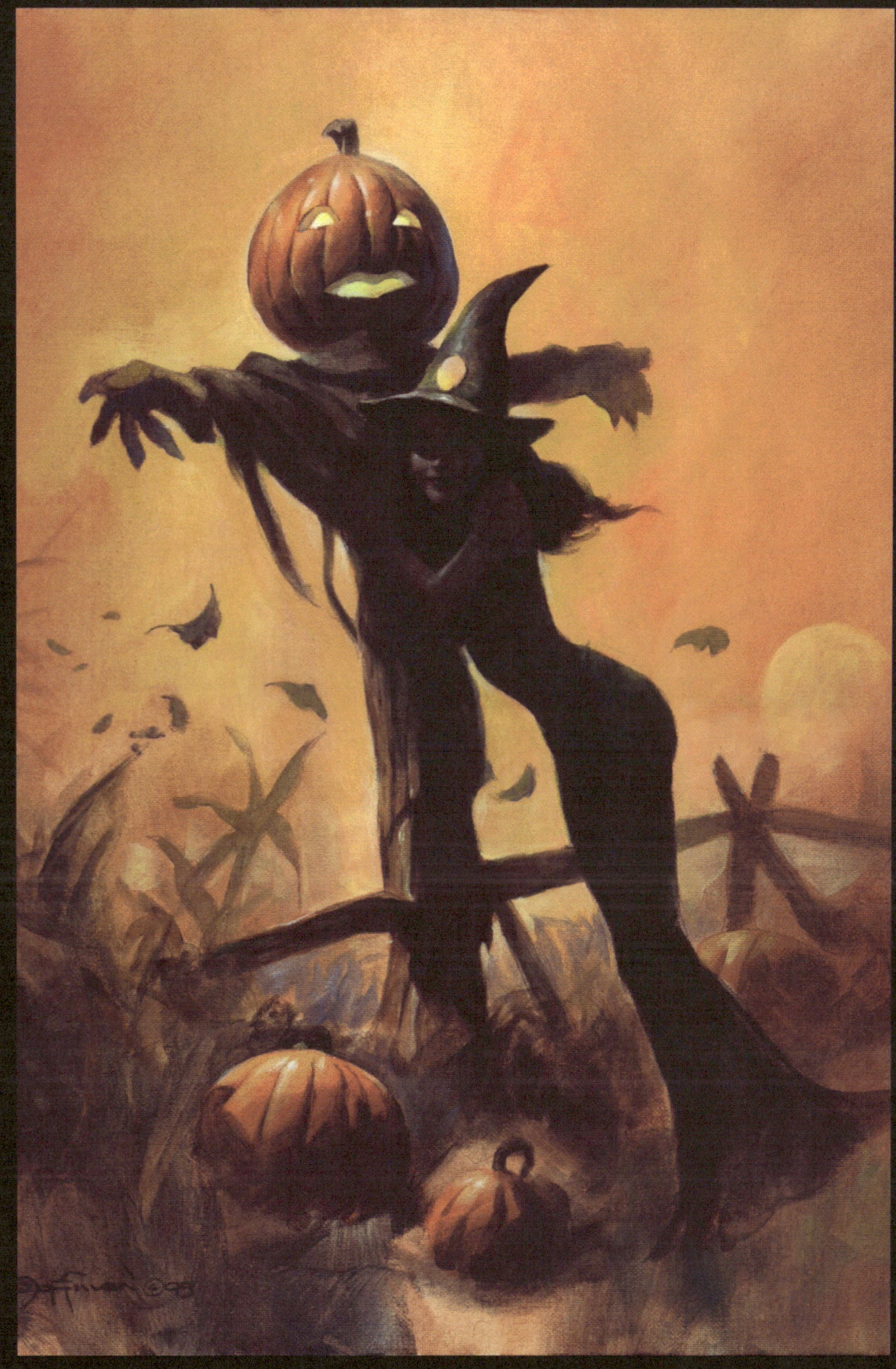

"SCARECROW GIRL"

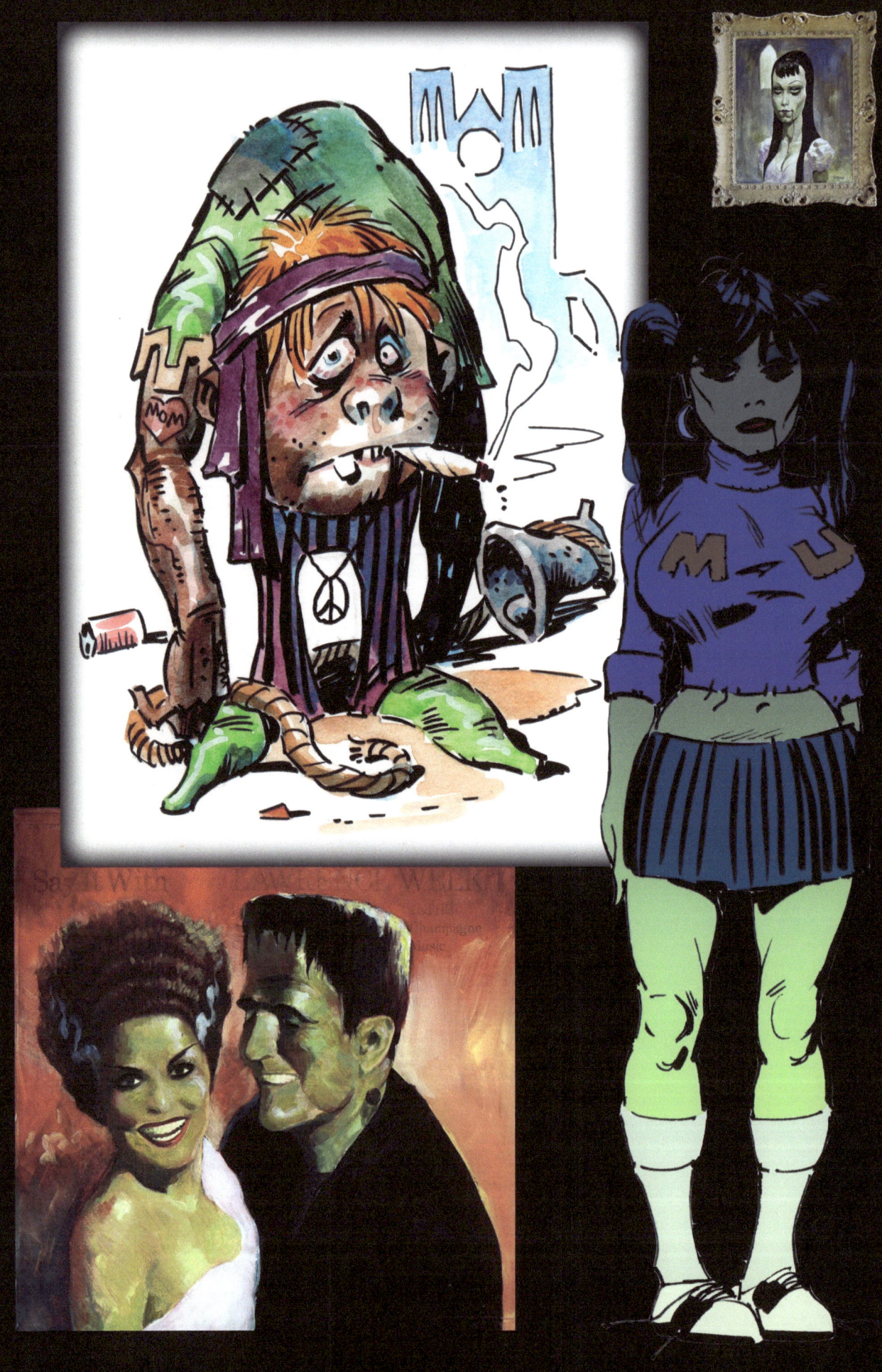

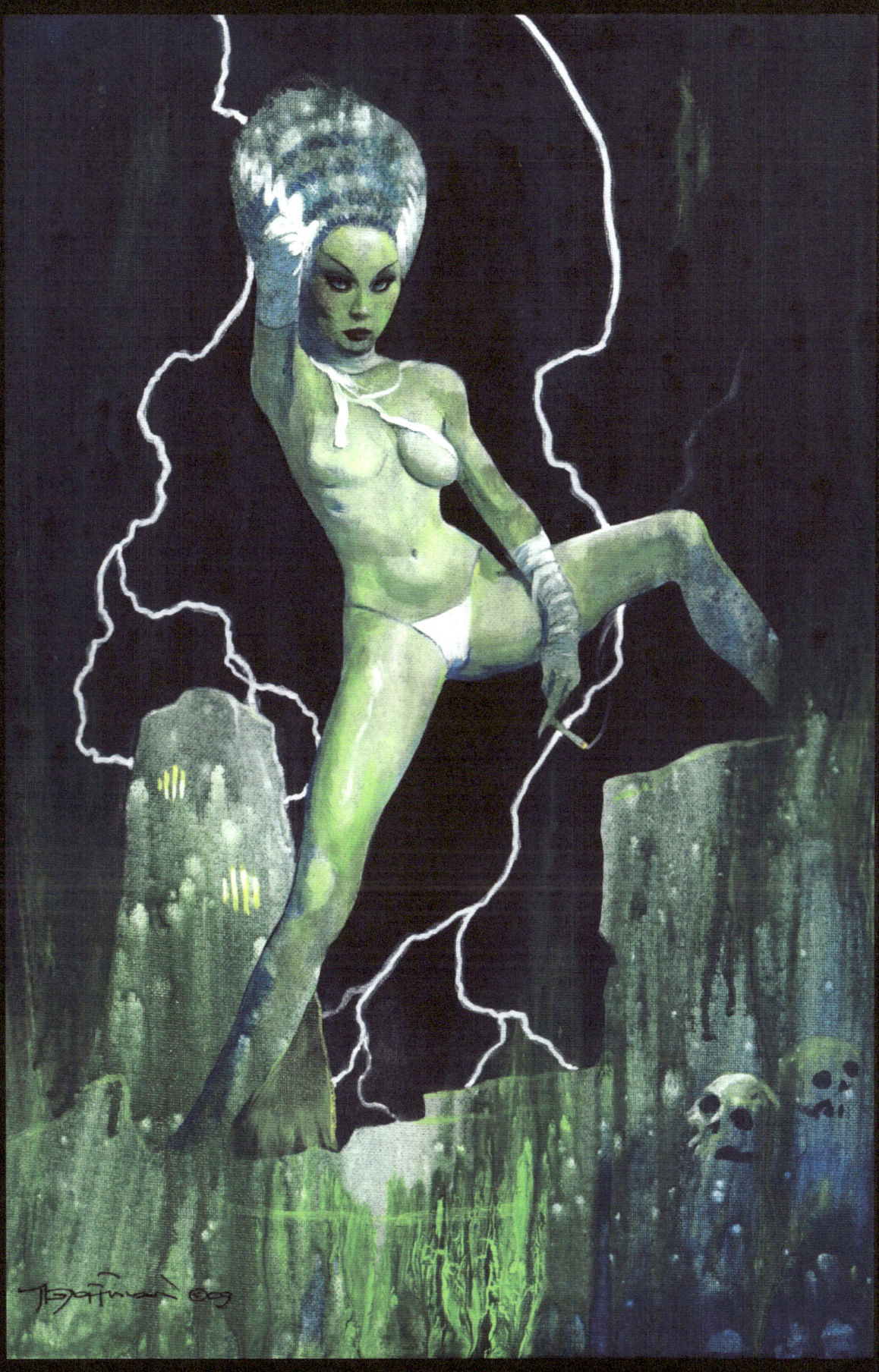

"THE BRIDE"

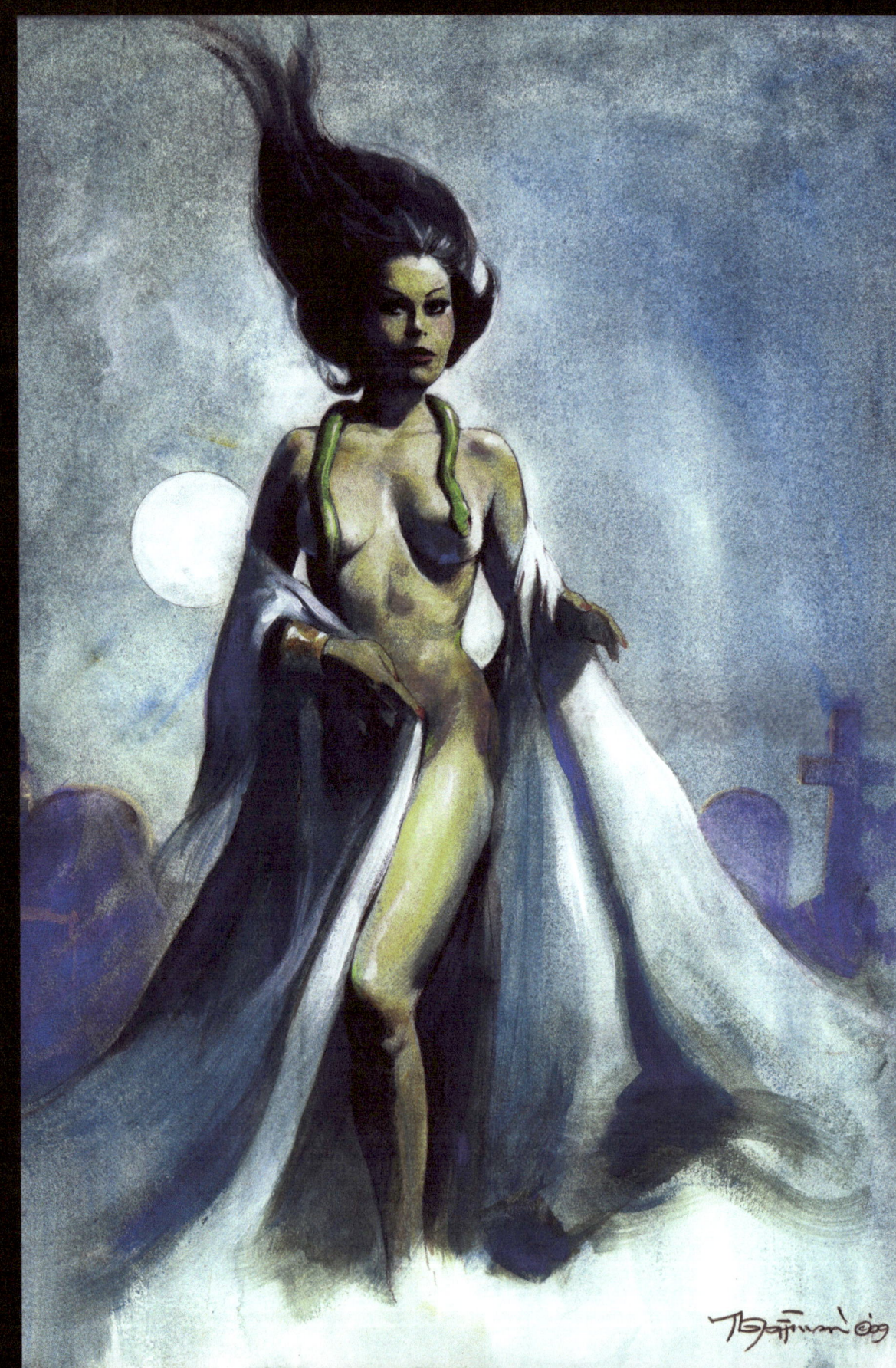

"SUCCUBUS"

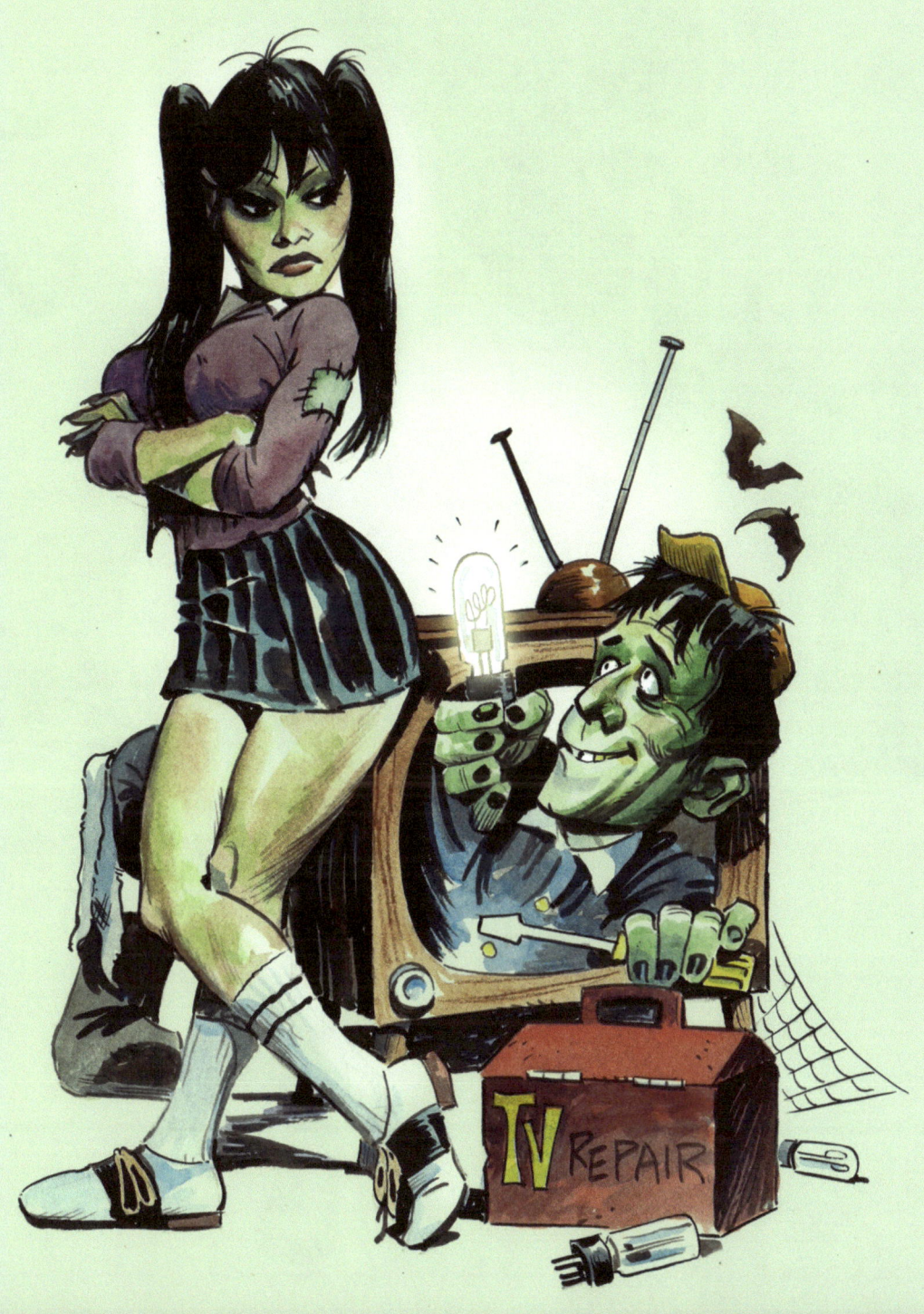

"T.V. REPAIRMAN"

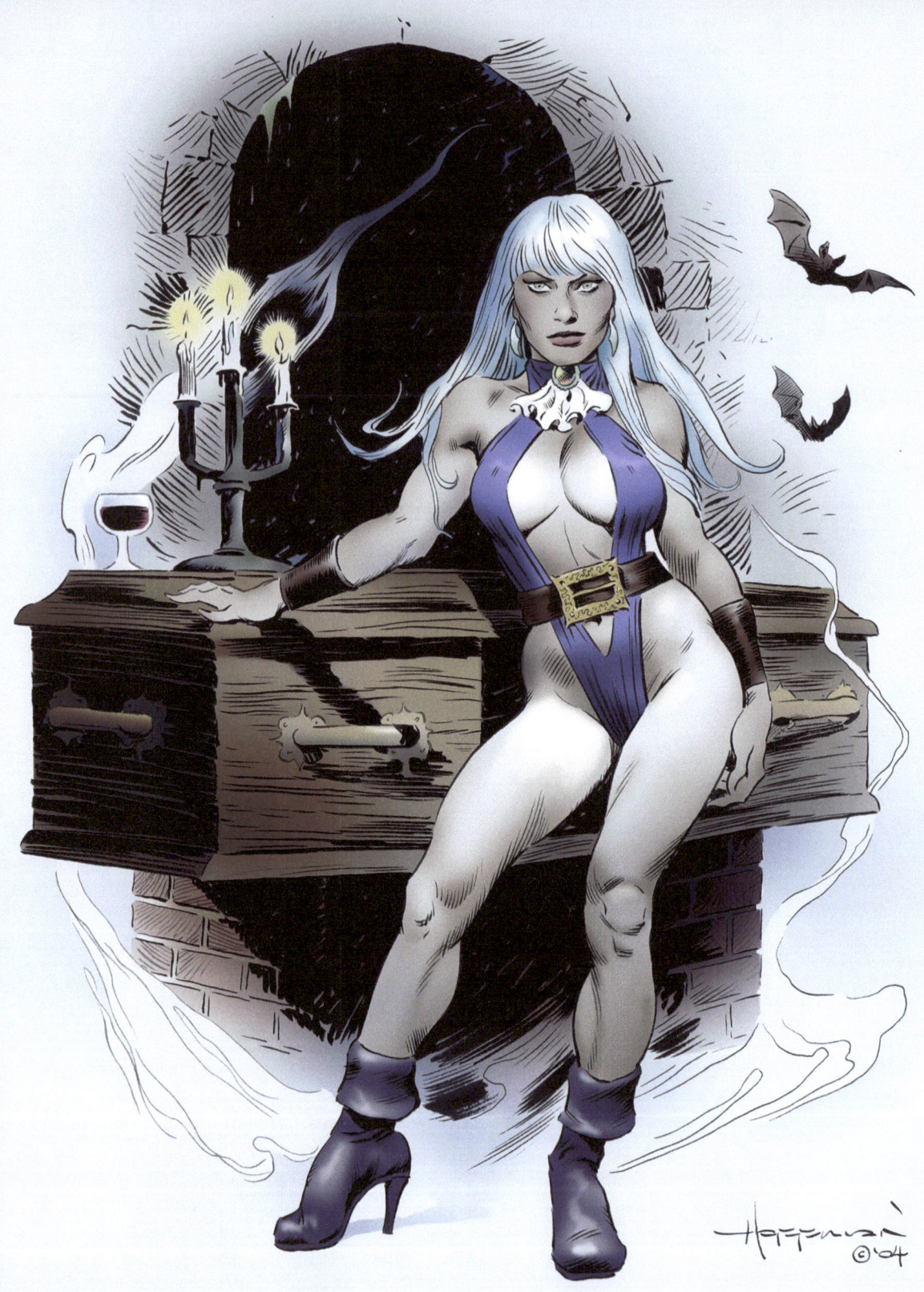

"VAMPIRESS COFFIN"

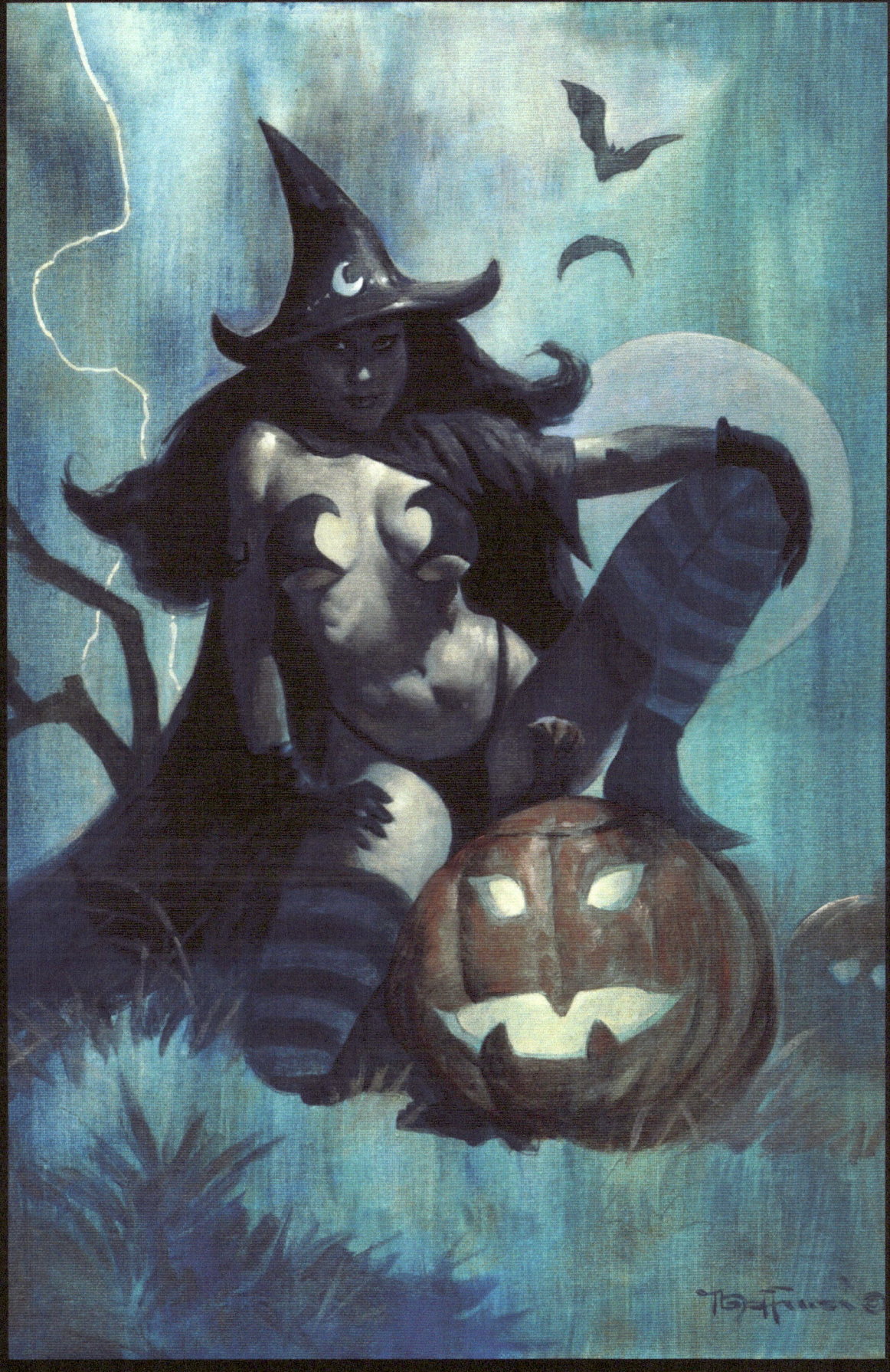

"WITCH SEASON"

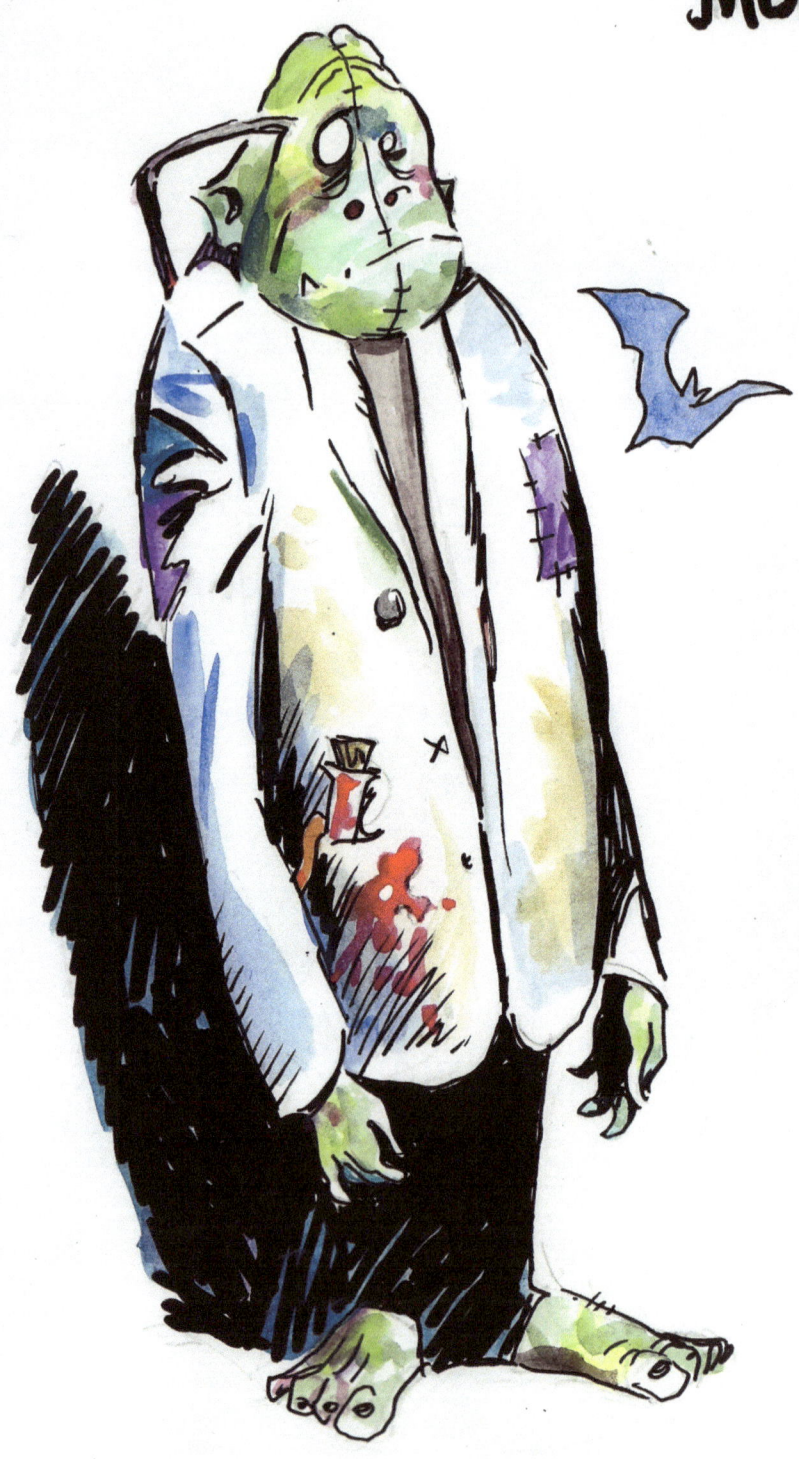

THE WELL-DRESSED
MONSTER

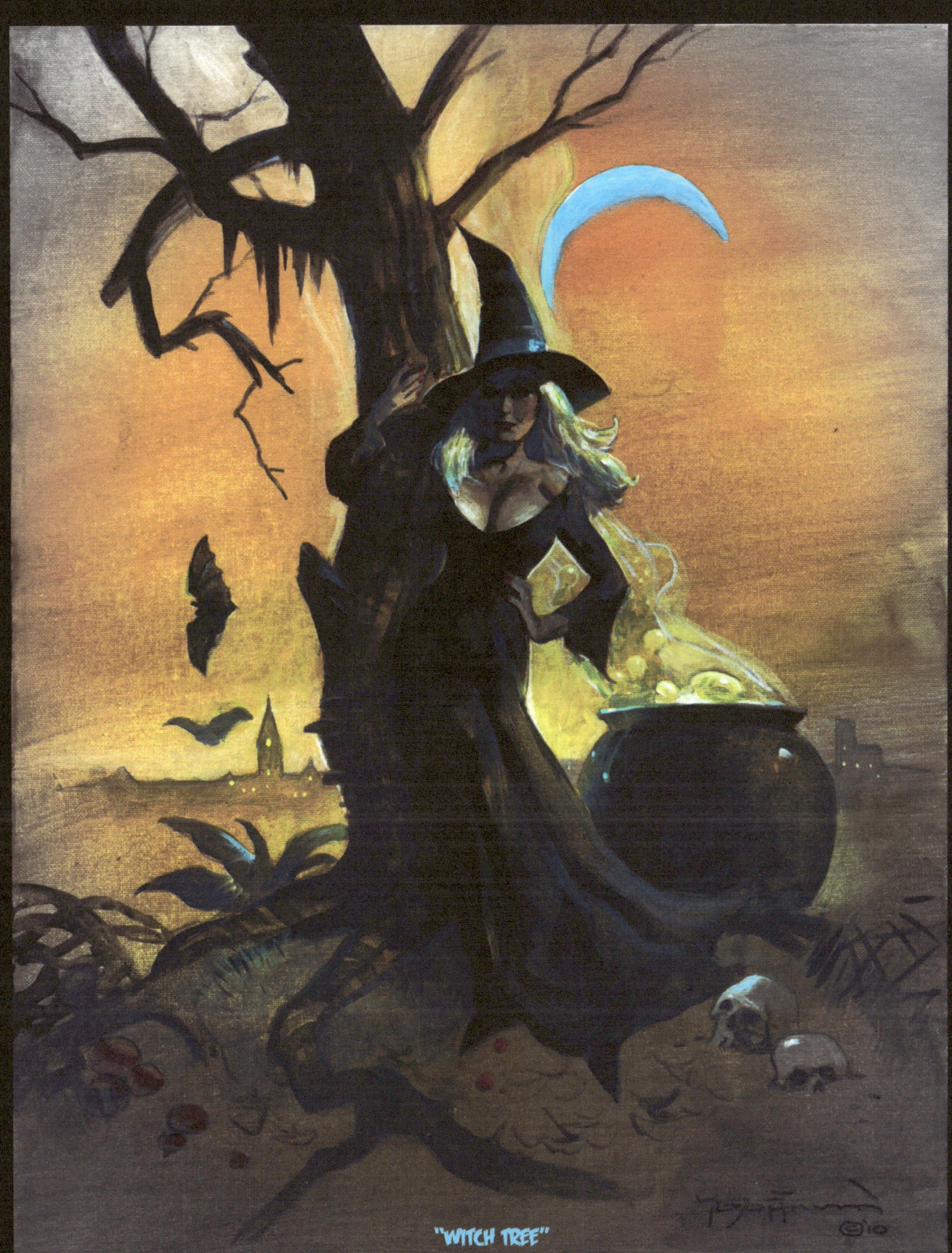

"WITCH TREE"

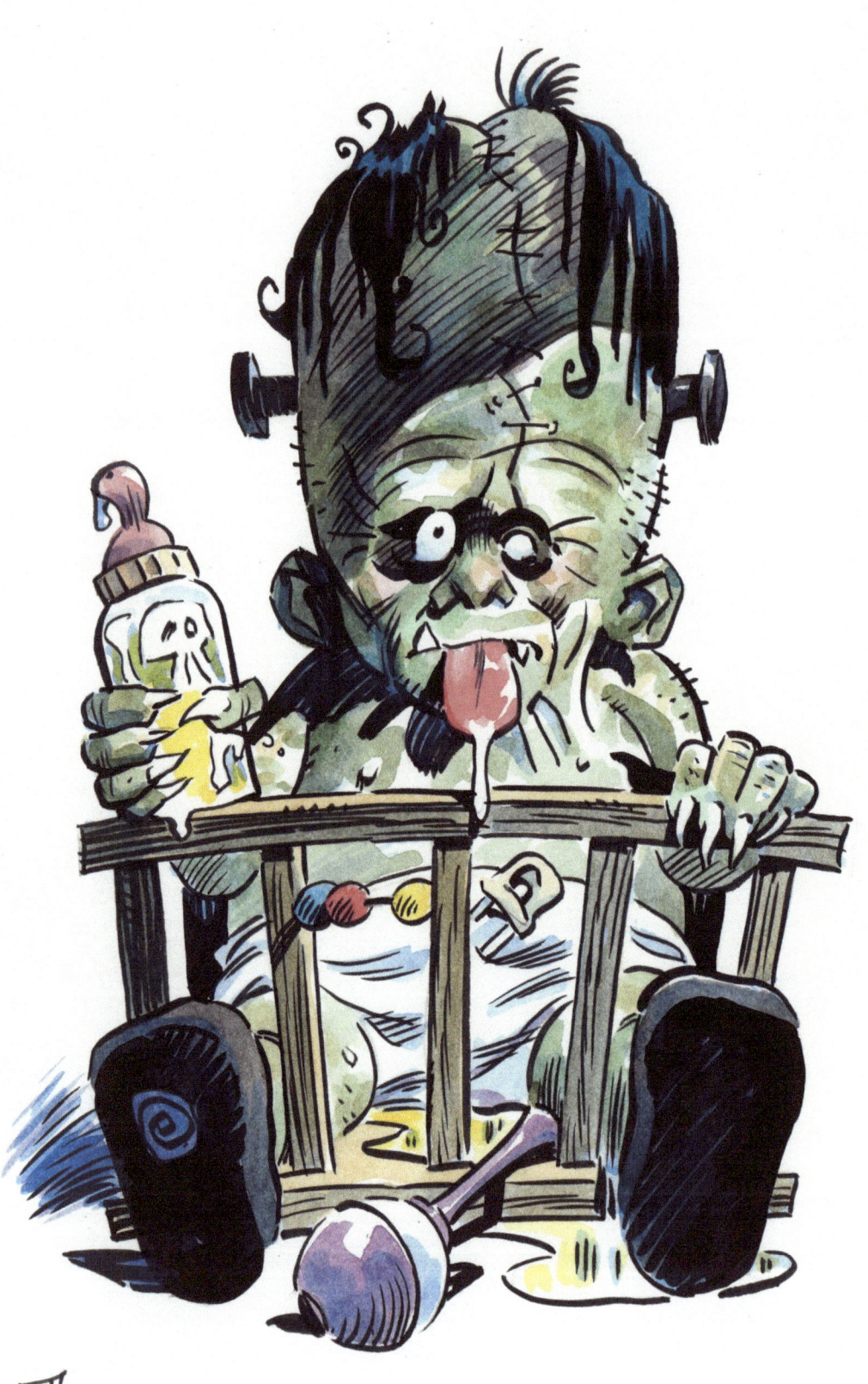

"BIGGER EVERY YEAR"

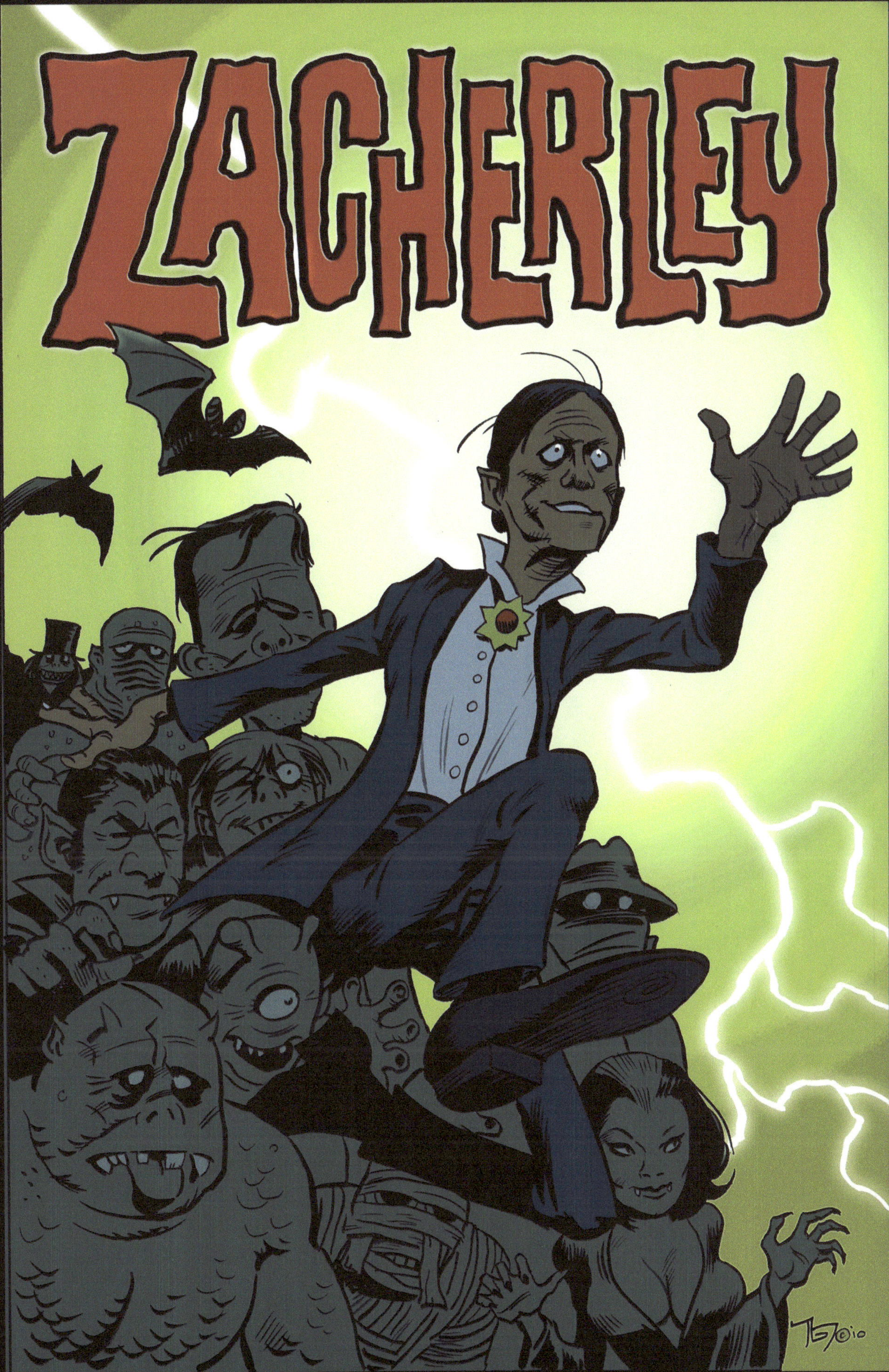
ZACHERLEY

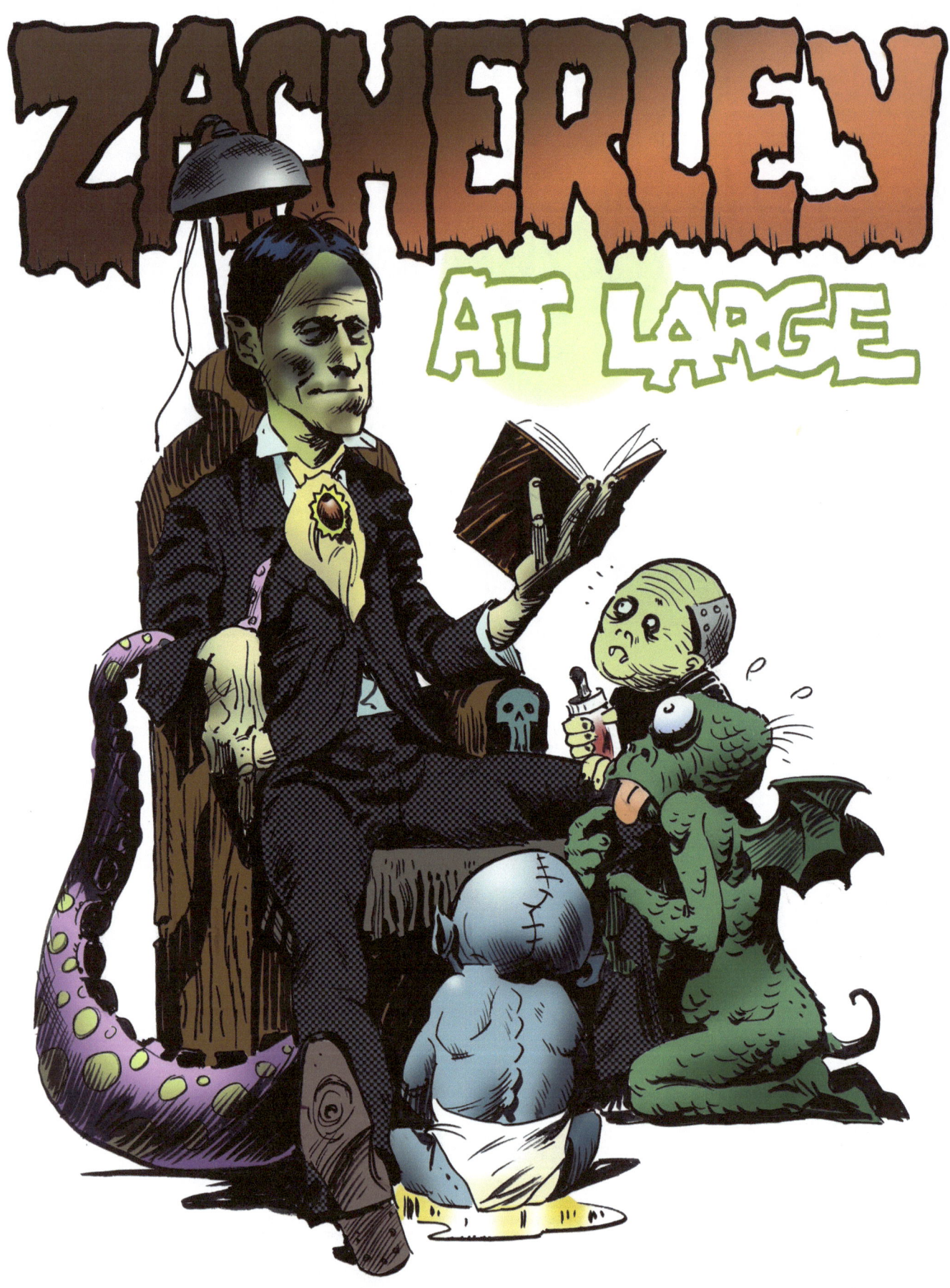

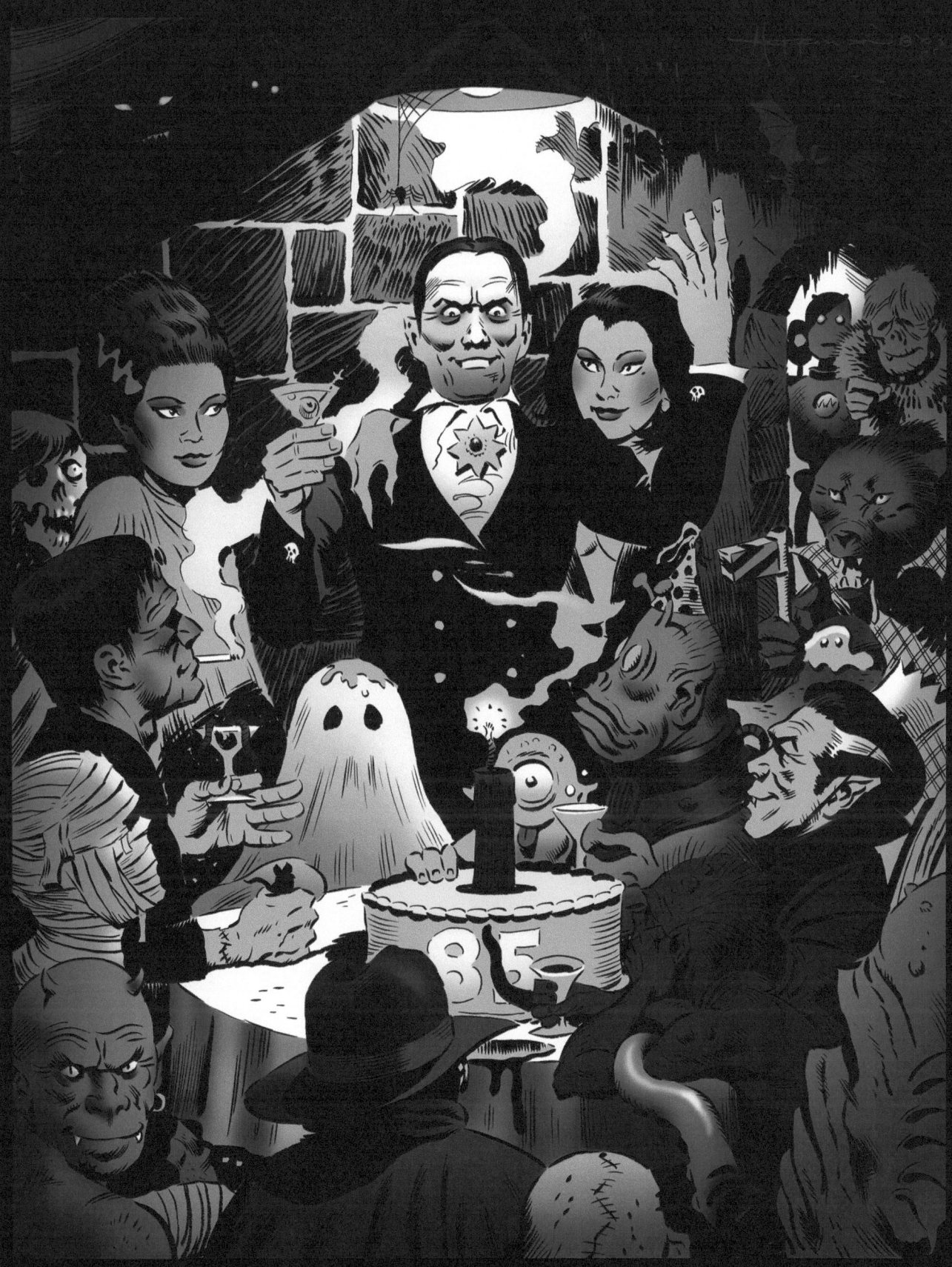

"ZACHERLEY BIRTHDAY"

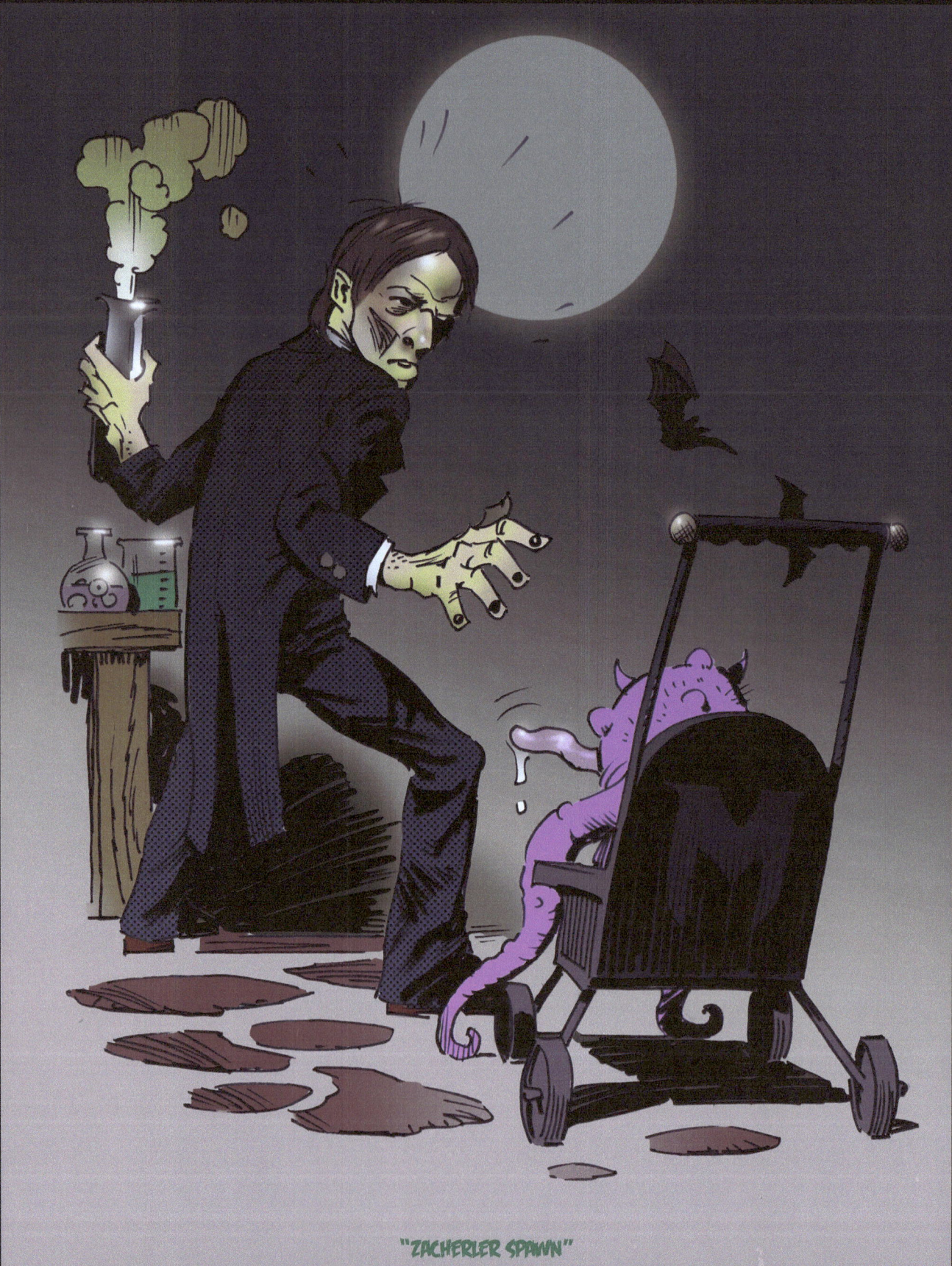

"ZACHERLER SPAWN"

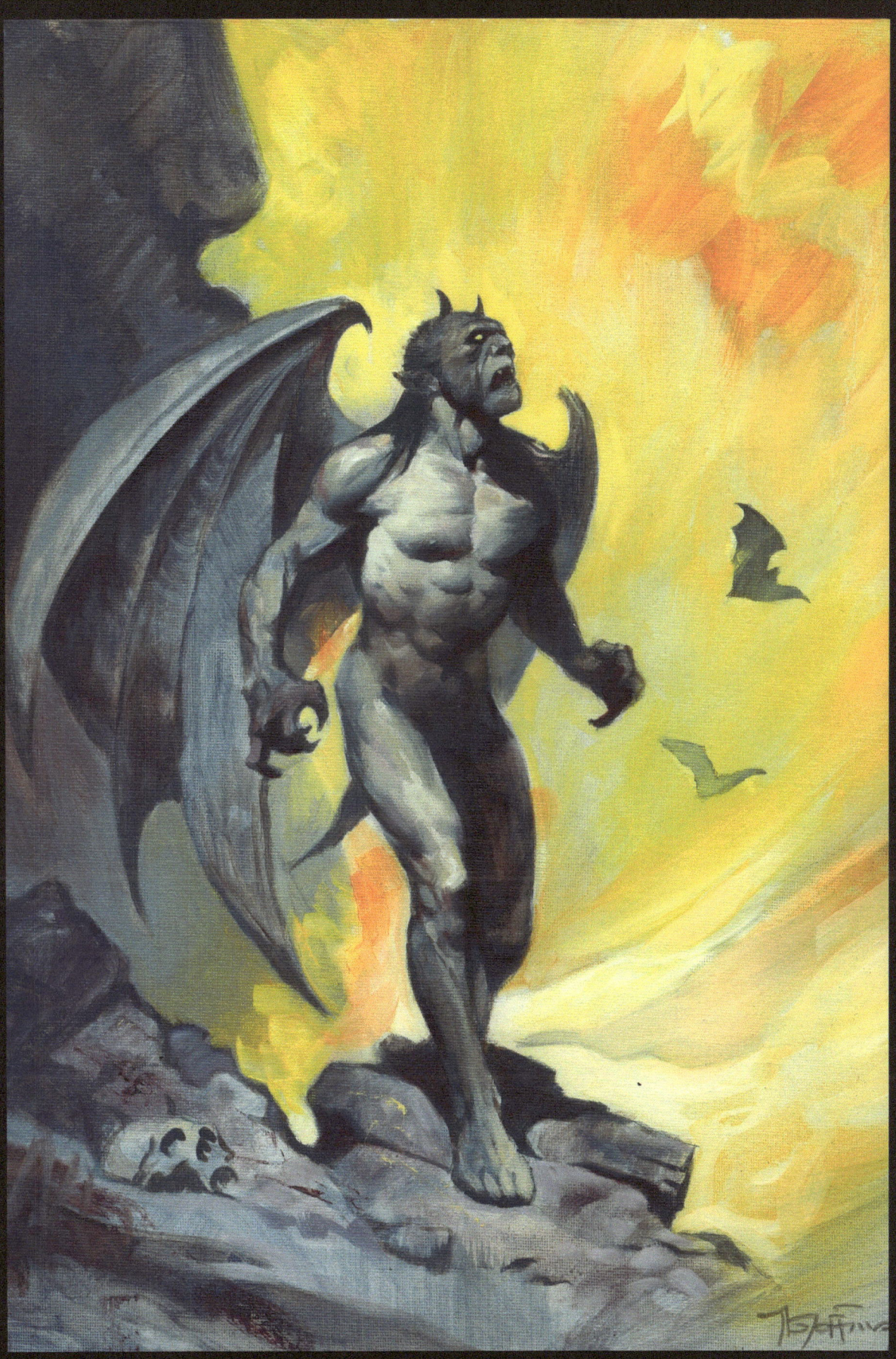

"DEMON DAWN"

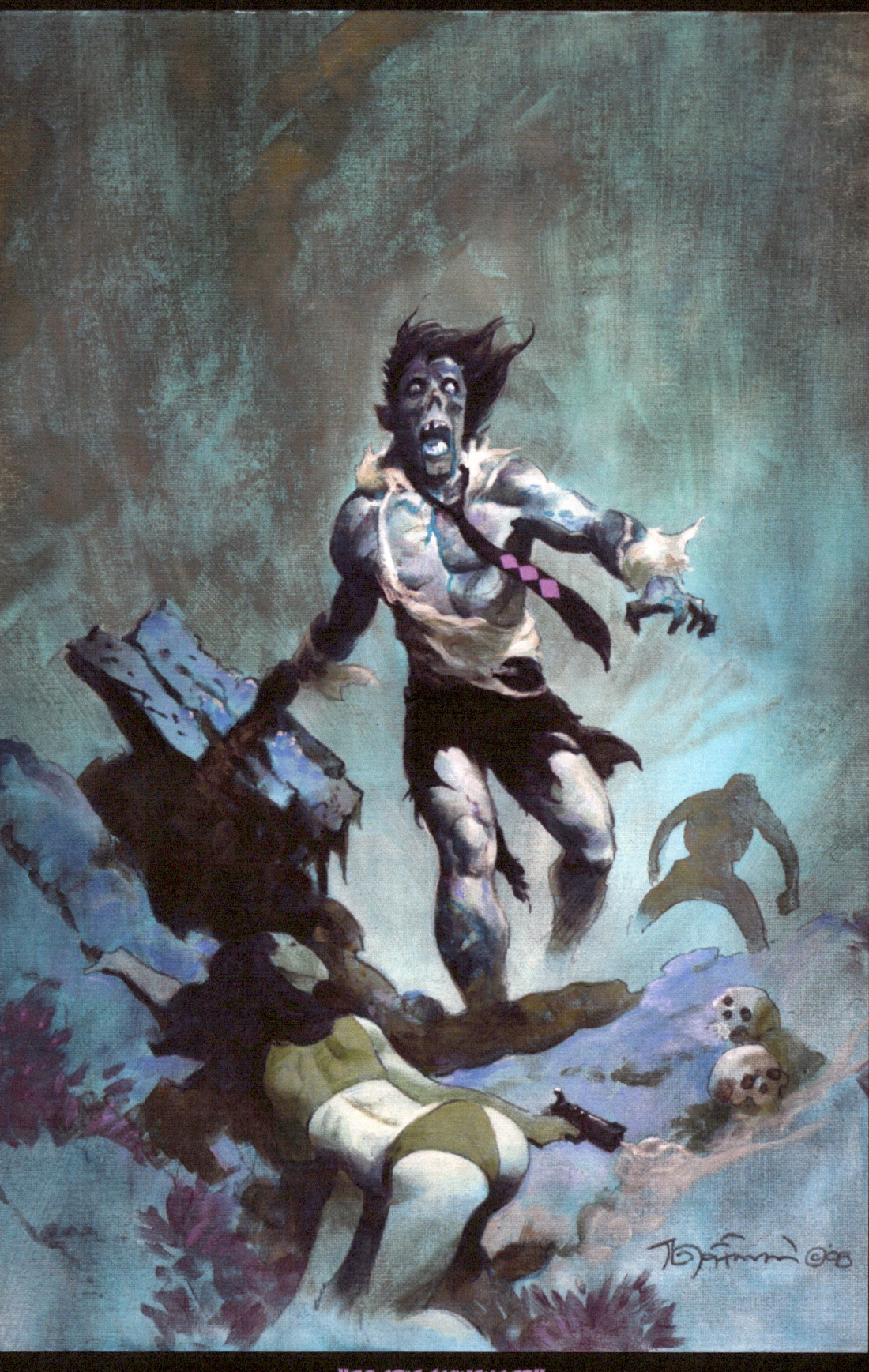

"ZOMBIE SCAVENGER"

www.ingramcontent.com/pod-product-compliance
Lightning Source LLC
Chambersburg PA
CBHW040749200526
45159CB00025B/1808